15 Steps to a Successful Remodel

How to Survive the Process

15 Steps to a Successful Remodel

How to Survive the Process

Peter A. Klein

Seal Rock Press

15 Steps to a Successful Remodel
How to Survive the Process

Worksheets and checklists have been included in this book to give you an idea of how much information you will need to gather in preparation for and during a remodel. Since these worksheets and checklists are probably not very useful in a 6" x 9" page, you may request the actual Excel and Word files from PeterAKlein.com, for use solely in your own remodel, not for commercial remodels, tenant improvement projects, design-build, or new construction. No use of any of these worksheets or checklists is permitted in any publication or commercial product without the author's written approval.

Published by
Seal Rock Press
Post Office Box 654
La Mesa, CA 91944-0654

Grateful acknowledgement is made to the following for permission to reprint previously published material: "Cost vs. Value," *Remodeling Magazine* © 2019 Hanley Wood, LLC (costvsvalue.com); "Preliminary Notice," "Proof of Notice Declaration," "Conditional Waiver and Release on Progress Payment," "Conditional Waiver and Release on Final Payment," "Unconditional Waiver and Release on Progress Payment," and "Unconditional Waiver and Release on Final Payment," Monk and DBug, LLC, and Construction-Business-Forms.com, © 2019.

Plans Used in the Cover Art, Copyright © 2019 LB Consulting

Cover Art Copyright © 2019 B. Asher Klein

ISBN: 978-1-7340343-0-1

Library of Congress Cataloging-in-Publication Data Available upon Request

I would like to dedicate this book to Nancy Cummins-Slovick, for being my editor, grammarian and partner; to my children, Kamala, Ben and Jacob, for encouraging me and putting up with me; to John Barker, for helping me believe in myself; to Yvette Souza, who made me realize I could do this; and to Walter Goodseal, for making sure I didn't miss anything.

Contents

List of Figures

It is not the beauty of the building you should look at;
it's the construction
of the foundation that will stand the test of time.

—David Allen Coe

Chapter 1. The First Step

A residential remodel may look as easy as drawing a few lines on some paper and hiring someone to build what has been drawn. That is a simplistic version of the process. There are many steps to get the you, the homeowner, from the initial concept to the final inspection.

15 Steps to a Successful Remodel: How to Survive the Process takes you, the reader, through the steps to achieve the desired finished remodel. Be forewarned that it is not a fast process, nor is it easy. If you want a successful remodel, complete each of the steps detailed herein. If it is worth doing, it is worth doing correctly. Follow these steps, and you should get what you want.

Several first steps need to be addressed: tell you about my background so you know my experience; explain why I wrote this book; give you an idea of what you will find within its pages; and discuss the sidebars you will see later in the book.

My Experience

An architect was I wanted to be in high school, so it was off to the University of Oregon. Philosophy and calculus did me in, so I joined the Navy to give me time to sort things out. After the Navy, I earned an associate degree in architecture and worked construction to see how designs were turned into buildings. Most of my time was spent in the carpentry and concrete trades, but I also spent time doing electrical work, plumbing, and many other trades, and occasionally spent some time as a drafter.

Over time I was hired to supervise various projects, most of which were residential, and then I gained a contractor's license and did a lot of remodels. After moving to San Diego, I went to work at Jack in the Box as a Senior Facility Engineer. This was like being a superintendent or contractor, except my projects could include all 1,000 restaurants spread across many states. I also earned a bachelor's degree in business administration.

Many of these projects required building permits, which led me to handling the permits for a sign contractor and then to go into business myself with Permits & More. I traveled up and down California and into Arizona for permits for a wide variety of projects. It was during this period that I wrote three articles on permitting for the trade publications *Sign Business* and *Sign & Digital Graphics* magazines.

Why I Wrote the Book

Around the same time I started doing permits for the sign contractor, there was a story on one of the local TV stations about a 92-year-old woman who signed a contract to have a sprinkler system installed in her yard. She thought the price was going to be $1,000. She wound up paying $2,225 for the work that was substandard at best. Luck was on her side. The contractor brought the system up to par and refunded $1,225 to her after the story was aired. This is not the norm in these types of cases.

That story lit a fire under me, and I secured a position at a local night school, teaching homeowners about remodeling. My lesson plans for that class became the start of *15 Steps to a Successful Remodel: How to Survive the Process.*

Stories about contractors who start jobs and then disappear are frequent topics for the business section of newspapers, consumer reporters, and investigative reporters. Many times, the home is left wide open. The homeowner and the contents of the house are exposed to the elements and to anyone who wanders by.

Skepticism should greet anyone putting door hangers on your front door, or in your mailbox touting a contractor, whether general or specialty. The same would apply to any door-to-door salespeople selling remodels. Some of these individuals are doubtless honest, hardworking people, but in my opinion, the deck is stacked against them. If they have a business card with a contractor's license number, a telephone, and a local address, maybe call them later.

In a nutshell, do not deal with anyone who comes knocking on your door and purports to be a contractor. The typical method of operation for the con men purporting to be contractors is to get a big down payment for whatever service they claim to be selling and promise to start several days in the future. They will do this to as many homeowners as they can in a few days and then leave town. Goodbye, money!

In the past decade, flipping houses has been very popular. However, several new homeowners who purchased flipped houses contacted me after being notified by the local code enforcement office that a section of the home they just purchased had unpermitted work, and the local jurisdiction expected the new homeowner to remedy the situation.

At least in California, any unpermitted work should have been disclosed to the buyer at the time of purchase. Buyers have the duty to investigate the property before making an offer or, in California, before escrow closes. Part of that investigation should include a trip to the building department to see if permits have been issued for all the work on the property. Also, in California, two disclosures are mandatory: the Real Estate Transfer Disclosure Statement and the Seller Property Questionnaire Statement.

If the new homeowners of a house with unpermitted work are lucky, they will just need to have plans drawn for the unpermitted work, obtain a permit, and make any corrections that are required, and the corrections are minor. If the unpermitted work was shoddy, the new owner could face tens of thousands of dollars of additional and unexpected expenses. Worst case, the new owner may be forced to remove the unpermitted work, at their own expense.

My experience has shown that working with code enforcement or the building department to correct the situation is a much better strategy than trying to fight them. Fighting will cost more time and money than working to put the situation in the past, as quickly as possible.

The ways to combat these swindlers and bad businesspeople are to make the public aware of how to use a contractor with a higher degree of confidence and to go a long way to ensure that the remodel will be a success.

The Content

While *15 Steps to a Successful Remodel: How to Survive the Process* may be considered a how-to book, you will not get ideas on Feng Shui or how to hang wallpaper. You will not learn how to build walls, hang drywall, or paint. This is a how-to book for the mind, not the hands.

15 Steps to a Successful Remodel: How to Survive the Process details the suggested steps every homeowner should know before starting a residential remodel. How much money you will need, who should design your remodel, and how to protect yourself and your property during the remodel are topics many people never consider before embarking on a remodel. Homeowners just know they want to remodel and proceed. This is not a wise way to undertake such a complex process.

Experience has shown that most people are unprepared for remodels. It makes selecting a contractor from the field of available contractors akin to navigating a minefield.

Contractors are notoriously poor businesspeople. In his book *How to Hire a Home Improvement Contractor Without Getting Chiseled*, Tom Philbin writes, "According to the Remodelers Council of the National Association of Home

Builders, some 80 to 90% of all contractors go out of business after five years."[1] That is a high failure rate!

15 Steps to a Successful Remodel: How to Survive the Process discusses the remodeling process and how you as a homeowner can go into a remodel with your eyes open. This book will take you through the remodeling process from start to finish. The starting and ending points may not be where you expect them. The goal of the book is for you to become aware of strategies for a successful home remodel so you can have your home remodeled without becoming a negative statistic.

Barring the very impulsive person, most of us do some comparative shopping before making big-ticket purchases. For instance, a lot of research is done before I buy a vehicle. My first stop is the library to look at back issues of Consumer Reports and their annual buying guide to see which models should be avoided and which ones have earned favorable marks. Next, it's out to the car lots to see what is available and affordable and fits my needs.

When thinking about a remodel, the needed research is spelled out here. The job of this book is to show you how to find the right designer, the right contractor, and the right remodel. It

---

[1] How to Hire a Home Improvement Contractor Without Getting Chiseled, Tom Philbin pg. 11

is my intention to convey enough information for you to remodel your home without becoming a victim.

By the time we finish going through each of these topics, you should be well armed and ready to remodel. Success is linked to how seriously you follow the concepts suggested in this book. As the old adage goes, "You can lead a horse to water, but you can't make him drink."

"Plan your work and work your plan." In a project as complex as a remodel, these are words to live by. Putting time into research and planning before the construction starts should reap big rewards during the execution. As an experienced project manager, I can tell you the most successful projects are the well-planned projects. It's up to you.

If you are planning to do the work yourself or act as an owner-builder, read the book anyway. Regardless of which path is chosen, the basic questions—what to build, how to get plans, how to select materials, how to obtain a building permit, and how to get the remodel built—must still be answered. All of that is covered in this book. Need to hire a specialty contractor? Just follow the steps for selecting a general contractor to select a specialty contractor. Regardless of the means to the end, a helpful book is *The Home Remodeling Organizer* by Robert Irwin.

Be forewarned: remodels are stressful. Be prepared for arguments with your partner, spouse, or significant other. If you can continue living in the home during the remodel, the change of routine may lead to changes in your sleep pattern. More stress. Exercise and meditation may help relieve some of the stress.

The Sidebars

Throughout this book you will find additional information in gray boxes (sidebars). These sidebars are divided into three categories. The first is the note, which is preceded with the graphic. The second is a tip, a bit of information related to the current topic. Tips are identified with the following graphic: , as in the "Call Before You Dig" warning. The third category contains information specific to California. California has a number of laws that differ from those of many other states regarding licensing of contractors. California-specific information is identified with the following graphic: CAL.

I am *not* a lawyer, and any references to contracts, contract law, contractor licensing law, and mechanic's lien law should not be construed as legal advice. These references are my opinions, accumulated from experience as a contractor, as well as research on the Internet and in a law library. My interest is to make you aware that there are laws governing contracting and contractors.

A final word of caution before we begin: remodels always seem to take longer than planned. Be prepared for a process that lasts several months. From your initial meeting with a designer until a Notice of Completion is recorded could take six months or longer. *Time put into planning is not time wasted. It is time well spent.* You will reap the benefits of planning during construction. Be patient.

I wish you luck and success with your remodeling projects!

You can use an eraser on the drafting table or a
sledgehammer
on the construction site.

—Frank Lloyd Wright

Chapter 2. What Will It Cost?

"What will it cost?" is the most commonly asked question about a proposed remodel. Most people ask it before they even know what the scope of their project will be. Until there are some concrete ideas of what might be built, there is no way to answer the question. However, most of the time it will cost more than you think!

Your Budget

The first thing that must always be done is to figure out how much you can afford to spend! This is the most critical part of the project. Without an in-depth analysis of what you can afford, you are not ready to remodel the home.

Are you planning to sell one or more investments to pay for the remodel? The sale of the investments may have to be timed just right, or the money needed may not be available. If you are short by 10%, can you still afford to do what you want or need?

If you come up short, are there ways you can adjust the scope of the work that will let you get most of the things you want? Maybe you can do your own painting or your own landscaping. Perhaps you can use a lower grade of cabinetry.

If you have champagne tastes and a beer budget, you're in trouble. Be realistic. Don't waste your time, the time of an architect, nor of any contractors, if you cannot afford the project.

To calculate your budget, be sure to include a contingency amount. If you decide you can afford to spend $50,000 and not much more than that, you should set the $50,000 as your limit and then deduct at least 10%. That 10% is your contingency.

In this example, your budget would be $45,000, and you would have a contingency of $5,000. You know you have $50,000, but only let the architect or contractor know you have $45,000. Give yourself a cushion.

One criterion that should be used in selecting a designer is finding a designer who is up-to-date on construction costs for your type of project. An architect should be able to help you stick to your budget. It may be the difference between a finished project that gives you what you want or forgoing the project altogether.

There is a saying in the remodeling business: "You never know what you are going to find until you get the walls opened." It usually happens. Designers and contractors may know their business, but they don't have x-ray vision. Having an architect who will help keep the design aligned with your budget will help ensure that your contingency is sufficient for your project.

How important is a contingency? Let's use a real-world example. In the last remodel of my house, we used up the contingency and a bit more. We replaced the bathtub, an ugly 1950s green. When the old tub came out and the contractor started the rough plumbing, he found that we had a corroded waste pipe at the tub's drain. It was 40-year-old cast iron pipe. We hadn't anticipated that cost.

When the contractor got to the master bath, we found that the waste pipe for the shower was also corroded. In both instances, he needed to jackhammer part of the slab, replace the pipe, and repour the concrete.

Together these two plumbing problems were not expensive. However, we later decided to have the old stucco sandblasted and then re-plastered. All that added up. That expense consumed the entire contingency.

By having a contingency, you prevent yourself from running out of money before you finish the project. An unfinished remodel can be unsafe, an eyesore, and an embarrassment. It creates bad feelings between homeowner and contractor, and it leaves a bad taste in everyone's mouths.

Let's look at where the money goes once a budget has been determined and the funds are set aside, including a contingency. The costs of remodeling are divided between direct costs and indirect costs.

Many items go into the cost of a remodel. Besides the construction materials, such as lumber, drywall, and nails, the quality of products can impact the cost. Although you can bring the cost down by picking the cheapest items, such as appliances, you may not be happy with the result.

Direct Costs

Direct costs are, by far, the biggest. Figure 1, the Home Remodel Budget Worksheet, lists the major cost categories you will encounter during a remodel. *(This worksheet, as well as other worksheets and checklists, is available in full-size format at no cost, from PeterAKlein.com.)*

In most cases, you will need to pay someone to design your remodel. If you use an architect—and I recommend you do—it will cost more than a building designer or drafter.

Engineering would cover the costs of an engineer to provide designs and calculations that are beyond the capabilities of an architect or designer. If you have a house on a steep slope, there may be engineering costs associated with calculating piers and beams for an addition that would not be needed on a more level lot.

Once a design has been selected, a government agency, a planning and building department, will need to be paid to get the plans reviewed and the permit issued. In California, the actual costs may be broken into a plan-check fee, a permit fee, and school fees.

The remodel cost will be the biggest single item. The total of the direct costs should equal the budget amount less 10%.

Excluded items are those things that the contractor has excluded from the scope of work in their proposal but that need to be done. For example, maybe you are going to do the interior painting yourself. You need to figure in the cost of the paint, drop cloths, brushes, rollers, sandpaper, and other items.

Home Remodel Cost Worksheet
Budget

Available Budget (90%)	$	
Contingency (10%)	$	
Total Budget	$	$0.00

Direct Costs

Design Fees	$	
Engineering Fees	$	
Permits	$	
Construction Contract	$	
Excluded Items	$	
Owner Provided Items	$	
Temporary Lodging	$	
Temporary Storage	$	
Fund Control	$	
Extras / Change Orders	$	
Other Consultant	$	
Other	$	
Total Direct Costs	$	$0.00
Budget - Direct Costs	$	$0.00

Indirect Costs		Per Month	Per Year
Property Taxes	$	0	0
Insurance - Fire	$	0	
Insurance - Earthquake	$	0	
Insurance - Property	$	0	
Utilities	$		0
Loan Payment	$		0
Total Indirect Costs	$	$0.00	$0.00

Figure 1 Home Remodel Cost Worksheet

A good way to start to get an idea of costs is to make a list of items you will need to include in the project. Say you want to remodel your master bathroom. Some of the items that top the list of what you will need are medicine cabinets, tile, a shower head, and a toilet paper holder.

Go to Lowes, Home Depot, or your local home improvement store's website and search for those items on your list. You will see that you can get a shower head and control valve and the toilet paper holder in the same style. Various styles from different manufacturers have varying prices. This exercise will help educate you about the costs you are about to incur. Do not include things like lumber, nails, plaster, or wiring.

Owner-provided items are the materials you, not the contractor, are providing. Maybe you have a special door you have already purchased or are going to purchase outside of the contract for the remodel. A possible way to save some money is to select the items that you want, buy them and store them in your garage until they are needed, or see if the store where you buy them will store them for you until you need them. Wait to do this until your plans are complete.

Lowes and Home Depot are not the only places to shop for these items. You can shop at local home improvement stores and small regional chains. Look for sales or discounted items that have the quality but not their normal price tag. By doing this you eliminate the contractor's markup on these items. Your legwork will reduce the contractor's time locating and acquiring supplies, saving you some money.

Extras and Change Orders are those items that are unforeseen, such as the plumbing problems I encountered in my last remodel. Extras and change orders vary so much that it is impossible to make any kind of prediction.

Fund control is an optional item. It is described in Chapter 13 Paying the Bills. It is having a third party make the progress and final payments for you. Using fund control will cost a small percentage of the contract price.

Temporary Lodging is also an optional item. If the remodel is so extensive that you must move out of your home, you need to figure that into the overall cost of the project.

Temporary Storage is another optional item. For example, if you have been using your attic for storage and then decide to convert it into a bedroom, all those items must come out and be stored somewhere. Maybe sell or donate them?

Once you know what your direct costs are, you can add them up and see how your total compares to your budget. You may find that you need to adjust your costs.

Indirect Costs

The last section of the worksheet lists the costs that are not part of the construction but are attributable to the project. These are the indirect costs. Property taxes may go up because of the remodel. Added square footage to the house will generally cause the homeowners' insurance to go up. Added square footage will probably cause the utility bills to increase. The heater has more space to heat, there are going to be more lights, and more floors to vacuum.

If you get a loan to pay for the remodel, you will have a loan payment each month.

Here are some other things to keep in mind. Bathroom and kitchen additions are expensive because of the plumbing. Second-story additions are more expensive than ground-floor additions. Custom materials will increase the cost of the project.

Be honest with yourselves. Establish a reasonable budget and stick to the budget. If you have a beer budget and champagne tastes, you're in for a rough time!

We shape our buildings; thereafter our buildings shape us.

—Winston Churchill

Chapter 3. The Money

Your house is wonderful. The remodel is going to make it a showplace. However, no one is going to remodel your home for free. Before you pick a contractor, you need to have your finances in good shape. The architect and the contractor are going to want to be paid.

Where do you get the money? Maybe you can get someone to give you the money, but probably not. Maybe you'll win a lottery, but probably not. That leaves you with three funding options—savings, investments, or loans—or a combination of these sources.

Savings

If you have been saving for a remodel, hopefully you have met your goal and can get the remodel you want. As you need it, you transfer the money from your savings account to your checking account. The drawbacks are that you lose your principal, there is no tax deduction, you no longer have a rainy-day fund, and if you run short you may not have a backup source of funds.

Investments

Maybe you have made a variety of investments to pay for your remodel. As with savings, you get the remodel, but you may have used up the principal. The drawbacks here are the same as with using your savings. In addition, you may have to pay capital gains tax on the investments you cash out.

Borrow from Life Insurance

If you have a large enough whole life insurance policy, you may be able to borrow against the accrued value of the premiums and investments in the policy. Borrowing against an insurance policy may offer a lower interest rate than the other types of loans described above. For further details, contact your insurance agent and your tax advisor.

Veterans Administration

If you are a disabled veteran and your disabilities are service connected, there are programs available to you through the Veterans Administration. Check with the nearest Veterans Administration office, your county or city veteran service office, or VA.gov/.

Loans

You may want to take out a loan to pay for your remodel. For many, this may be the only way to get the money to make the remodel happen. The advantages of a loan are that you don't have to diminish your principal as you would by dipping into a savings account or an investment account. Second, you may be able write off the interest if you do it right. Third, you have no capital gains taxes to pay.

The information on loans discussed here is from mortgage brokers I have known for several years. Only a brief overview will be given of the loans you can use for financing a remodel. The loans covered in this chapter are a construction loan, an FHA 203(k) loan, first-mortgage-loan refinancing, second-mortgage/home-equity loan, home-equity line of credit, reverse mortgage, and contractor financing. Keep in mind that the better your credit rating and the higher your equity, the better your loan options. Shop around for a mortgage broker who will work for you, not for their commission.

Let's look at the types of loans available to you.

Construction Loan

A construction loan is a short-term loan, generally for the term of the construction project. Construction loans are more common for new construction than for remodels. The interest rate for a construction loan is based on the prime rate. If you get a construction loan, *you must* convert it to a permanent loan after the remodel is finished. You will have to do some research to find financial institutions that make construction loans. Financial institutions that make them for new construction may not make them for remodels and vice versa.

If you go the route of getting a construction loan, The lender will send an inspector to the project each time a payment request is made. This ensures that the project is being built to the plans and specifications the property owner has agreed to. In most cases, the inspector will be from a third party, hired by the lender. The lender's inspector may spot some work that is substandard and want the work corrected before any more funds are disbursed.

FHA 203K Program

The United States Department of Housing and Urban Development (HUD) has a program called a 203(k) Rehab Mortgage Insurance. While the name of the program sounds like an insurance program, it is in fact a mortgage program. The home must meet some requirements to qualify, including a certain level of energy efficiency. Here is HUD's description of the program: "The Section 203(k) program is FHA's primary program for the rehabilitation and repair of single-family properties. As such, it is an important tool for community and neighborhood revitalization, as well as to expand homeownership opportunities."[2]

The 203(k) program is available through FHA approved lenders. There are 203(k) consultants as well to help you with the process. To find one of these consultants, go to hud.gov/program_offices/housing/sfh/203k/203k--df.

First-Mortgage Refinancing

If you have enough equity in your house, you may be able to refinance your mortgage, possibly up to 80%, and use the money you are able to cash out to pay for the remodel. As this is written, interest rates are close to the lowest they have been in decades. Most lenders are happy to refinance for a remodel because the remodel will enhance the value of the property. As an added benefit of a first mortgage, the interest may be tax deductible.

Home-Equity Line of Credit

A home-equity line of credit sounds like a good tool for those of you who have a good credit rating and a good amount of equity in your house. Most lenders will lend to 70% of value. The interest rate you will pay, which is based on the prime rate, will

---

[2] U.S. Department of Housing & Urban Development, HUD.gov/program_offices/housing/sfh/203k.

be governed by your credit rating and the amount of equity you have. Equity lines of credit are generally for ten-years' duration.

The advantages of an home-equity line of credit are that you pay only the interest on the amount used, not the whole line of credit, and the interest may be tax deductible.

The disadvantage of a home-equity line of credit is that the payments are usually interest only, for ten years. You must remember to pay down the principal. Second, if you want to refinance your first mortgage, you cannot use the home-equity line of credit for at least twelve months prior to refinancing.

Reverse Mortgage

For homeowners aged 60 or older, a reverse mortgage is an option. An advantage of a reverse mortgage is that it cannot be frozen. For example, say a reverse mortgage was taken out for $200,000, the value of the property at the time the loan was initiated. Then the market drops, and the property's value goes down to $100,000. With a traditional mortgage, the borrower is "upside down." This is not the case in a reverse mortgage.

A reverse mortgage is a non-recourse loan. A non-recourse loan is defined thus: "Non-recourse debt is a type of loan secured by collateral, which is usually property. If the borrower defaults, the issuer can seize the collateral but cannot seek out the borrower for any further compensation, even if the collateral does not cover the full value of the defaulted amount. This is one instance where the borrower does not have personal liability for the loan."[3]

In the aftermath of the 2008 recession, the lines of credit and equity loans were frozen so that the borrower could not draw out any more money. Not so for reverse mortgages.

Contractor Financing

Some contractors may offer financing for the remodels they perform. These loans may not be to your advantage. The interest rates could be higher than would be charged by a bank, credit union, or mortgage broker. They will probably have additional charges such as points, closing fees, and more, that may be waived if you use a different source of financing. Be sure to contact your tax advisor as to what is tax deductible.

General Considerations

Three important things to consider. First, never take out a loan that requires a balloon payment. Second, never get upside down on a loan; that is, never borrow more than 100% of the appraised value of the property. Third, if you take out a loan with an adjustable rate, make sure that you are aware of how much the principal is reduced with each payment. You may find

---

[3] Investopedia.com, 2020.

that the principal reduction is considerably less than with a fixed-rate loan. Any of these things could hurt you.

Don't take the first option you consider. If you are considering a loan, shop around. Compare interest rates and other costs you will need to pay to consummate the loan. For example, one lender may charge points, but another may not charge any points, or they will charge fewer points. The points are money out of your pocket.

Check with your financial advisor or your tax advisor for advantages and disadvantages of each of these financing options for your circumstances. What may be a prudent idea for one household might be unwise for another.

We are building up slowly. We want to get it right.
—Drew Sharp

Chapter 4. What Are You Going to Build?

Okay, you've definitely, sorta, kinda made the decision to remodel your house. Does that sound familiar? Some of you may know what you want in a remodel. Others haven't a clue. They just know they want to change their home, but they are unsure what they want. Remodeling means different things to different people. In my own experience, one thing seemed like the best idea at the start of the planning and we wound up with a different remodel—but one that satisfied our needs.

Concepts

Maybe old bathroom and kitchen plumbing could use replacement. Maybe the family is growing, and another bedroom or bathroom is needed. Perhaps the children have moved out and it is time to convert a bedroom into an office or hobby room. There are lots of possibilities of things that can be done. At a loss for ideas? Try *Sunset Magazine*, *Better Homes and Gardens*, and other publications of that type for ideas. Two other sources of ideas and photographs are Houzz.com and Pinterest.

Another way to get ideas is to inspect your home. Are there areas that just don't work for your way of life? Is there dry rot or termite damage that needs to be repaired? Does the exterior trim need painting? These are things that could be made part of a remodel. For help in inspecting the home, you will find a wealth of ideas in *The Complete Home Inspection Handbook* by Norman Becker.

Visit home shows in the area. Visit model homes in your area. Any of these things may trigger a thought that can become the start of a remodel plan.

Several years ago, we gutted our kitchen and put in new windows, cabinets, flooring, and appliances. Within six months we were talking about adding space to our home. We had three sets of preliminary plans worked up. We talked to six building designers, two architects, and several general contractors. We knew we wanted to add on, but we didn't know what we wanted. We wound up working with architect Jerry Lecko, who was able to translate our confusion into a design that matched our needs to the letter.

Once a rough idea has been developed, look at your neighborhood and determine if the remodel will price the home out of the market. If the home had to be sold one year after the remodel is finished, would the asking price to be too much for the neighborhood to support?

Types of Remodels

To my mind, there are two types of remodels: facelifts and bone surgeries. They are very different in their scope.

Facelifts

A facelift is doing cosmetic things such as repainting, installing new drapes, or replacing the facings on the kitchen cabinets. These are basic, simple, easy projects—the kinds many of you could do on your own. I refer to these as home improvement projects. If the house in question is one you don't plan to own for a long time, stick to facelifts. Otherwise, the costs may never be recouped when the house is sold. It depends on the market, which takes into account the neighborhood, city, and state in which the property is located, as well as the national economy.

Bone Surgeries

Bone surgery projects involve opening walls, changing the plumbing, adding rooms, foundation work, and so on. These types of projects take longer to complete and to recoup the investment.

Whichever path is taken, don't make the remodel a monument to your ego.

If the reason for remodeling is to make the home more marketable, be sure to put money in the right places. For 2019, "Remodeling 2019 Cost vs. Value Report" (see Figure 2)[4] found just three projects recouped their cost: one in the San Diego area and two in the Pacific Region.

The best was a garage door replacement, which recouped 123.8% of its cost[5] in the Pacific Region.[6] Number two was also in the Pacific Region. This was manufactured stone veneer at 110.4%. A manufactured stone veneer is thin stone or brick on a backing that is applied to the side of a building. At the bottom end of the scale nationally was a master-suite addition. This remodel recouped only 50.4% of its cost. This also had the worst return on investment (ROI) in the Pacific Region.

According to this same report, the information shows that what works in one area of the country may not work in another. Figure 2 has the breakdown for San Diego, the Pacific Region, and the Nation.

---

[4] Remodeling 2019 Cost vs Value Report (CVVR), (Hanley Wood, LLC, 2019); complete data from this report can be downloaded free at CostVsValue.com.
[5] Remodeling 2019 CVVR, Remodeling.hw.net/cost-vs-value/2020/.
[6] Remodeling 2019 CVVR.

In San Diego County, replacement windows returned 83.7% of their cost, which is better than in most other areas of the country.[7] In San Diego County 15 years ago, window replacements would pay for themselves. Nationally, window replacements don't come close to recouping their cost. The best returns in San Diego are for garage door replacements, at 108.8%.

A distant second is a grand entrance (Fiberglas) at 89.8%.[8] A grand entrance is a fancy door. It should be noted that the figures shown above are based on the house being sold one year after the remodel.

Remodeling for the resale market? Stick to facelifts or home improvement projects. Remodeling to make the home a better fit to the way you live is better if you plan to stay put for several years.

Looking at the table of cost vs. resale value brings another term to mind. That is *home improvement*. How does a home improvement project differ from a remodel?

---

[7] Remodeling 2019 CVVR.
[8] Remodeling 2019 CVVR.

San Diego, CA

PROJECT TYPE	Job Cost	Resale Value	Cost Recouped	Job Cost	Resale Value	Cost Recouped	Job Cost	Resale Value	Cost Recouped
Bathroom Addition | Midrange	$ 58,557	$ 34,566	59.0%	$ 55,051	$ 37,264	67.7%	$ 47,427	$ 28,726	60.6%
Bathroom Addition | Upscale	105,321	64,853	61.6%	99,868	65,863	66.0%	87,704	51,000	58.1%
Bath Remodel | Midrange	24,993	16,779	67.1%	23,548	17,728	75.3%	20,420	13,717	67.2%
Bath Remodel | Upscale	76,394	48,242	63.1%	72,734	48,548	66.7%	64,743	38,952	60.2%
Bath Remodel | Universal Design	39,126	20,100	51.4%	37,339	24,955	66.8%	33,374	20,868	62.5%
Minor Kitchen Remodel | Midrange	26,128	21,803	83.4%	24,950	21,723	87.1%	22,507	18,123	80.5%
Major Kitchen Remodel | Midrange	75,447	48,128	63.8%	72,513	49,384	68.1%	66,196	41,133	62.1%
Major Kitchen Remodel | Upscale	148,965	89,662	60.2%	143,333	89,429	62.4%	131,510	78,524	59.7%
Master Suite Addition | Midrange	160,094	115,500	72.1%	151,211	105,965	70.1%	130,986	77,785	59.4%
Master Suite Addition | Upscale	328,187	197,893	60.3%	309,768	175,519	56.7%	271,470	136,820	50.4%
Deck Addition | Composite	23,005	18,833	81.9%	21,858	18,392	84.1%	19,150	13,232	69.1%
Deck Addition | Wood	17,201	15,213	88.4%	16,511	14,491	87.8%	13,333	10,083	75.6%
Backyard Patio	65,003	43,317	66.6%	63,109	40,045	63.5%	56,906	31,430	55.2%
Entry Door Replacement | Steel	2,056	1,548	75.3%	1,986	1,549	78.0%	1,826	1,368	74.9%
Grand Entrance | Fiberglass	10,042	9,015	89.8%	9,568	8,147	85.1%	8,994	6,469	71.9%
Garage Door Replacement	3,865	4,204	108.8%	3,785	4,685	123.8%	3,611	3,520	97.5%
Window Replacement | Vinyl	18,949	15,857	83.7%	18,152	14,793	81.5%	16,802	12,332	73.4%
Window Replacement | Wood	22,495	19,696	87.6%	22,016	18,368	83.4%	20,526	14,530	70.8%
Siding Replacement	18,970	14,359	75.7%	18,409	15,515	84.3%	16,036	12,119	75.6%
Manufactured Stone Veneer	9,867	7,964	80.7%	9,507	10,499	110.4%	8,907	8,449	94.9%
Roofing Replacement | Asphalt Shingles	25,904	20,071	77.5%	25,476	19,806	77.7%	22,636	15,427	68.2%
Roofing Replacement | Metal	44,910	30,673	68.3%	44,406	29,608	66.7%	38,600	23,526	60.9%

CONFIDENCE LEVEL: 95% +/-3.6   CONFIDENCE LEVEL: 95% +/-1.4

Figure 2 2019 Remodeling Cost vs. Value Report

Remodel vs. Home Improvement

A remodel is defined as a construction project undertaken on a residential property that either adds square footage or alters the interior space. Remodels include projects such as adding a family room, enlarging a kitchen or family room, gutting and refurbishing a bath or kitchen, converting a garage into livable space, adding an enclosed patio or sunroom, or adding a pool.

A home improvement project, or facelift, is a project that does not alter the layout or structure of the residence. Home improvement projects include painting the house inside and out, re-stuccoing, reroofing, installing rain gutters, refacing kitchen cabinets, replacing windows, and adding a "Solatube" skylight.

There is a third classification, which is an accessory dwelling unit.

Accessory Dwelling Units (ADU)

So, what is an accessory dwelling unit? These units are called *granny flats, junior units,* or *companion units.* In most jurisdictions they are officially named accessory or auxiliary dwelling units (ADUs.) Here is how the City of La Mesa, California, defines it: ADU "shall mean an attached or a detached residential dwelling unit on the same lot as an existing dwelling unit zoned for single-family or multi-family uses that provides complete independent living facilities for one or more persons, including permanent provisions for living, sleeping, eating cooking, and sanitation on the same parcel as the primary dwelling unit is situated...."

A granny flat is like separate apartment on the same lot as an existing home. The granny flat may be attached to the existing residence or stand alone. The granny flat must be self-contained in that it must have areas for living, sleeping, eating, food preparation, and sanitation (toilet, sink, and shower.) There are additional restrictions, such as the square footage and additional parking.

In California, because of the housing shortage, the State has mandated that the various jurisdictions ease the process for approving granny flats. For instance, the requirement for additional parking spots is waived if the granny flat is within one mile of public transportation. Also, in San Diego County, the permit fee is waived in unincorporated areas.

There appear to be no restrictions on who may live in a granny flat. The residents could be your in-laws, your college-age children, other college students, or anyone else who passes your background check.

There may be a monetary downside to granny flats. In some jurisdictions, a transportation impact fee is imposed on the property as an additional fee at the time of permitting. This fee is often imposed for properties within one mile of public transportation. If you are considering a granny flat, check with the jurisdiction that will be issuing your building permit to see if they impose such a fee, or any other fees, specifically for accessory dwelling units.

Rules, Rules, Rules

Before starting the design of the remodel, there are a myriad of laws, rules, and codes to consider, not the least of which are building codes. Before that, you must determine if the project being considered will violate any neighborhood limitations.

Most neighborhoods were created when a developer bought a piece of land and created many lots out of the one big piece of land. This is called *subdividing*. The builder then put in the utilities, built the streets, and built the homes.

Homes may be single-family dwellings, condominiums (condos), co-op apartments, or planned-unit developments. When the developer created the subdivision, they drew up a document called Covenants, Conditions and Restrictions (CC&Rs.) CC&Rs run with the land, which means that even when a lot or residence is sold, the CC&Rs *may not* be ignored. They transfer with the title, cannot be separated from the land, and must be followed.

Condos and similar developments often have a Homeowners' Association (HOA.) The HOA has its own bylaws and rules, written by the developer and their lawyers at the inception of the project, to protect the development and the property values.

The CC&Rs, and HOA rules are often more restrictive than most zoning laws that may be in force in your community. The only city I know that doesn't have any zoning laws is Houston, Texas. Check your area to determine if CC&Rs or an HOA is a governing entity that controls what you can and cannot do to your property.

Once it has been determined that the project being considered will not run afoul of the CC&Rs or an HOA, it is a good idea to see if anything about the project conflicts with local planning regulations and zoning laws.

Zoning and Planning

Most local city and county governments have zoning laws and planning regulations. The idea behind these laws and regulations is to keep "like land uses" together. This provides orderly neighborhoods. There is also a transition from one use to a different use. In most cases, it keeps single family residences away from factories.

The zoning laws and planning regulations add further restrictions to what may be built within each zone. For instance, many residential zones have height limitations.

These laws and regulations also dictate the minimum lot size, the maximum lot coverage by the building, and the setbacks. Maximum lot coverage is the maximum area of a lot a building may cover. As an example, if a lot is 20,000 square feet and the maximum lot coverage is 60%, then the building, a house in this example, may not exceed a footprint of 12,000 square feet. In many cases this limit is imposed only on the ground-floor coverage.

The property line along streets is not normally located at the edge of the pavement nor at the back of the sidewalk (when one exists). (Locating the actual, legal property line may require that the lot be surveyed so that the designer knows just where the property lines are and how the existing structure is situated on the lot.)

Setbacks keep buildings from abutting each other as well as from abutting sidewalks. Many residential neighborhoods in San Francisco have residences abutting each other and are tight to the sidewalk. Across the Bay, however, most houses in Berkeley and Oakland have a buffer between each other and are set back from the sidewalk.

Side yard setbacks tend to be the same on both sides of a building unless one side faces a street. Corner lots tend to be bigger because the setbacks tend to be deeper on the side-street side.

One remodel many people consider is converting a garage to living space. In many single-family residential zones, if a garage is to be converted, then parking space must be provided for each car that can no longer park in the garage, *and* that parking must be behind the setback line. This is an example of how zoning laws impact what can be built.

Add to the various rules, laws, and regulations at the local level, state laws could impact a remodel. As an example, in California, whenever a swimming pool is installed, a fence must be erected around the pool to keep small children and other non-swimmers out of the pool and prevent accidental drownings.

These laws and regulations limit what a homeowner may do to a residence. Many cities now prohibit the parking of motorhomes in front yards. RVs must be parked in a side yard or in an off-site storage yard. These limitations have three goals: health and safety,; aesthetics, and property values.

There is no limit to the number of ideas of what a remodel will be. Keep in mind that some restrictions limit what may be built, imposed by the developer and the local zoning laws. You may also want to factor in what the real estate market is doing.

A goal without a plan is just a wish.

—Antoine de Saint-Exupery

Chapter 5. The Designer

The steps you have taken to this point have prepared you to speak with someone about converting your ideas, the budget you've developed, and the materials you have selected, into a set of drawings. You need a designer.

The person you select to design your remodel should follow these steps:

1. Interview you to find out what your ideas and budget are.
2. Write a proposal/contract.
3. Have you sign the contract.
4. Measure the existing dwelling, as well as analyze and document the existing structural conditions and other existing systems, and overall construction.
5. Inspect the lot: are there any obstacles to the project concept?

6. Research zoning laws, CC&Rs, and building codes for your locale.

7. Make a preliminary drawing or set of drawings.

8. Review the preliminary drawing(s) with you.

9. Make design changes from your input.

10. Review with you the construction documents required for your project.

11. Draw a complete set of construction documents.

12. Review final construction documents with you.

Steps 7 through 10 may be repeated several times before you see what you want. The first drawings will be simple until you start to see the layout you want.

A preliminary design will assist you in making some decisions about your project and will help prioritize your thinking. A preliminary design represents the ideas you have agreed upon with the designer. The preliminary design should include a floor plan and one exterior elevation. The preliminary design will not be enough information for accurate biding or for obtaining a building permit. It will be enough for a general contractor to prepare a preliminary estimate. Preliminary estimates from a couple of contractors will give an indication of the gap between your ideas and your budget.

For my last remodel, we had a preliminary design drawn, had some changes made to it, and then had three contractors give us rough estimates for the job. After we reviewed the bids, we scaled back the scope of the work and came up with a remodel we could afford that satisfied our needs. We added an office and reconfigured another part of the house so our sons could have their own rooms.

One criterion that could be used in selecting a designer is finding someone who is up-to-date on the cost of residential construction. A designer should help you stick to your budget. A designer who works to keep your project within your budget may be the difference between a finished project that gives you what you need or forgoing the project altogether. Ask designers you are considering, to provide at least a rough cost estimate of their design.

Who should do your design work? There are five possibilities: architects, building designers, drafters, contractors with in-house designers, and you.

Architects

In my opinion, an architect is your best option. In most cases, you will get a better product from an architect. Most architects have spent at least five years in college learning their craft. Several additional years are spent working for a licensed architect. It is like an apprenticeship. Each state's architectural licensing board governs the time spent as an apprentice. A grueling multi-day exam administered by the state is the last part of the licensing process. The term *architect* is a professional title granted to individuals who have shown a minimum level of competency to provide responsible design services while protecting the health, safety, and welfare of their clients and the general public.

Architects are taught design as well as structural engineering and the use of materials. They receive a thorough knowledge of building codes as well. They know where to go to research for such things as setbacks and CC&Rs.

Which architect should you use? It should be someone who balances the artistic with the practical. For a modest remodel, you don't want someone who has a great flair for designs that cost above comparable projects to build. On the other hand, you don't want an architect who is very practical yet has no flair. You want an architect who listens to you and can translate your ideas onto paper.

My friend Jerry, an architect with his own practice, spends about 25% of his time working with other architects. Jerry sometimes assists them in converting very impractical designs into designs that are reasonable to build but still aesthetically pleasing. Jerry designed our latest remodel.

Jerry was a perfect fit for us. My wife had many questions, along with my concerns. Jerry was patient and answered our questions. He listened to us and kept us within

our budget. When the remodel was complete, the new room
didn't "stick out like a sore thumb." And we liked it!

Building Designers

In California, you may still be able to find a licensed building
designer. The state agency that licenses architects also
handles licenses for building designers. Building designer
licenses were eliminated in the 1970s. However, those with a
valid building designer license may still practice. Other states
may have a similar professional title or license.

Building designers in California were limited to designing
single family dwellings, residential duplexes, and commercial
buildings of two stories or less. In terms of education and
experience, a building designer ranks between an architect and
a drafter. Much of my time as a drafter was with a building
designer who was excellent at designing pleasing, functional
homes.

Related to building designers are designers. These tend
to be people who have attended architectural school, or who
may have a degree in architecture, but have yet to pass the
state exam for architects.

Drafters

The next step down the scale in ability, education, and training
are drafters. In a traditional architectural firm, the architect does
the design work and the drafters, under the architect's

supervision, draw the plans. The drafters may be apprentice architects, students studying architecture, or simply drafters. To me, using a drafter is almost like acting as your own architect.

You will find a wide variety of abilities of drafters. Some are very capable people who produce nice designs and draw clear plans. At the other end of the spectrum are drafters who produce work that is messy, lacks detail, and doesn't provide clear instructions to the builder.

There tend to be few laws governing someone setting up a business as a drafter, if they do not represent themselves as an architect or engineer or use the terms *architectural* or *engineering*. You don't know what level of competency you will find, unless you use an architect.

If you go with a building designer or drafter, it is a good idea to check into their background. They should have at least four years' experience in an architectural firm. The circumstance is that they left the last architectural firm they worked for as a job captain. A job captain is someone in an architectural firm who has more experience than, say, employees who are just out of school, and they are managing one or more projects and several drafters. Also, since most building designers and drafters are not licensed, they should have a close relationship with at least a structural engineer.

The less experience a building designer or drafter has, the less desirable they are for you to hire.

Contractors with Designers

Some general contractors have an architect or designer on their staff. The contractor will try to use this as an additional selling point. It may work to your disadvantage. Since the designer is an employee of the contractor, the designer has the contractor's best interests in mind, not yours. The designer is going to design what the contractor can build. What the contractor can build may not be what you want built. In addition, the designer may be good, but the contractor is not. Or vice versa.

Using an architect or designer in a contractor's office may make it difficult for you to get copies of the completed construction documents so that you can get several competitive bids from other contractors. Another thing that may happen is that the contractor or designer will tell you that you are getting the plans (construction documents) at a special, low price. In fact, if you use that contractor, you will pay for the plans (construction documents) via inflated construction costs.

Draw-It-Yourself

In the movie *The Addams Family*, Gomez Addams says to a judge, "They say that a man who represents himself has a fool for a client. I am that fool!" If you are so inclined, you could draw the plans yourself.

However, how well do you know the building codes in your area? Can you put down enough detail to satisfy the local building department? Do you have a drawing board or a computer with a CAD program and a plotter? Do you have the knowledge and tools to do it yourself? Can you be objective about what you draw? Designing and drawing a remodel is not the same as high school mechanical drawing. Can you write a set of specifications that will protect you?

Selecting Your Designer

The goal of the design phase is to find someone to transfer your ideas to paper (the construction documents) so a contractor can understand the scope of the project, prepare an accurate estimate, and successfully build your project with a minimum of confusion or ambiguity. An architect (or a designer) may cost more than a drafter, but it is money well spent.

It is your decision, but using an architect will give your ideas the analysis of a professional. An architect will provide some fresh ideas. An architect will make sure your project is designed to comply with the local building codes. If you make such a request, an architect is capable of performing periodic job inspections on your behalf to make sure things are proceeding according to the construction documents. It will be an additional charge, but if you are unfamiliar with construction, it may be a worthwhile investment.

Should you use an unlicensed designer? In my opinion, you must look harder to find a good one. For our latest remodel, we talked to several unlicensed designers, and weren't happy with any of them.

Like most other things, the recommendation of a trusted person is the best way to select an architect. Ask people you know, who have built a new home, remodeled their home, or have had construction done at their business, for names of architects.

Another way to locate an architect is to contact the American Institute of Architects (AIA). Not all architects are members of the AIA. Many good architects do not belong to the AIA.

You can visit the AIA's website (AIA.org) and read their information on selecting an architect. Most large cities have chapters of the AIA. Call the AIA chapter closest to you. They will get some general information from you and then give you a list of names of architects with experience in projects like yours.

Interview several architects before you decide. Get an idea of their personalities, how they work, and whether you are comfortable with them. Most will not do any design work for you until you sign a contract with them for their services. Get references to get an idea of the architect's abilities and personality. Talk to some of their previous clients. If possible, see if you may visit some of the architect's previous projects.

If you are able to visit some of an architect's previous work, think about the following questions: Does the remodeled area blend into the rest of the building? How are the transitions from old to new areas inside the house? Do the traffic patterns created by the design of the remodel make sense? If the remodel doesn't look like a remodel, you have found a viable candidate for your designer.

You might also visit the architect's office and look at some of the other projects they have done. It might trigger some thoughts of things you could include in your design.

CAD

One of the inroads technology has made in the field of architecture is the advent of computer-aided drafting (CAD) systems. The use of a CAD system does not reflect on an architect's design abilities or professional competence. Using a pencil, a T-square, and a triangle on a piece of paper is more satisfying for some architects. It makes them feel more connected to the design. It is an intangible that is part of the profession.

Rarely will your designer come up with the perfect design for you on the first draft. To speed the process, give the designer a list of things that are important to you. To further assist the designer, prioritize the items on the list, as some items may conflict with others.

Fee Schedule

One way to help you filter the information you get from the designers is to ask each designer for a fee schedule based on the proposed drawings. The fee schedule should give you an idea of the drawings the designer feels are necessary for your project. The fee schedule should also take into account the project's complexity and include the costs for outside consultants, such as specialty engineers.

The fee schedule may include an estimate for the permit process. While the permit fees may be easy to calculate ahead of time, it is becoming more and more difficult to figure out how long the permitting process will take, especially in California. Many jurisdictions are experiencing a high employee turnover and therefore lower competency levels, which leads to longer permit-processing times.

The four building blocks of the universe are fire, water, gravel and vinyl.

—Dave Berry

Chapter 6. Making Selections

Decisions are at the heart of remodeling. Two quotes from two friends describing the planning process: "Remodeling is decisions, decisions, decisions" and "I didn't know there were so many decisions to make!"

Each of those decisions affects the final product. The sooner they are made, the better. Decisions made at the last minute may be rushed and therefore flawed, expensive, or both. Decisions made after the contract is signed may lead to change orders and cost increases.

Selecting materials is a tradeoff between cost and quality. You need to find the proper cost level for your budget. As we have all heard, "You get what you pay for!" Some things are more likely to impact cost than others.

Let's look at something as ordinary as door hardware. The two big brands for door locks are Kwikset and Schlage. A Kwikset doorknob with lock will cost about $48.00, and a Schlage doorknob with lock will cost $49.00. Not much of a difference. Match what is already in the home or select the one you feel has better quality.

In most cases, the color of an item won't cost more, unless item X comes in red, white, or blue and you want yellow. Then you have a cost increase for special order items, if available.

Appliances are an area where cost might be the deciding factor. They range from apartment grade, such as Roper, to Thermador with lots of bells and whistles and a much higher price tag. Want very expensive? Restaurant-grade appliances, such as Wolff, are very pricey. But they will all cook your dinner.

You, the homeowner, will not have much input on the additives in the concrete, drywall, or stucco, other than the stucco color. On which items should you want or need to make a decision? You should have a say not only in the things that affect the aesthetics, safety, energy efficiency, and aging in place, but also in the ordering of materials.

Aesthetics

What types of things affect the aesthetics of the remodel? Here are a few things to consider: colors for paint, stucco, roofing materials, appliances, plumbing fixtures, electrical trim, window frames, and glass color. Most of these items won't impact price unless special-order items are selected.

If each surface, wall, floor, and ceiling is considered, that should give a sense of some the decisions that must be made, as well as items that affect the aesthetics. The Room Finish Schedule in Figure 3 is useful for tracking these decisions. *(This worksheet, as well as other worksheets and checklists, is available in full-size format at no cost, from PeterAKlein.com.)*

Don't forget plumbing and electrical fixtures. A toilet can be purchased for $113.00 at Dixieline in San Diego. Or you can upgrade to one for $1,000.00 or more. (These prices are in San Diego County and will vary by location and time.) Other items that will impact costs are doors, flooring, tub and shower enclosures and surrounds, light fixtures, and cabinetry materials. Let's consider doors for a moment, and let's narrow it down to just front doors.

Doors. A door can affect the aesthetics of your home and also the indirect costs that result from the remodel. Eliminating all the other factors, doors come in two types: hollow core and solid core. As their names imply, the interior of the door is either hollow or solid, respectively. A hollow-core door should never be used as an exterior door, as it will take less weather abuse and fewer bumps and bangs. Its thermal efficiency is less, which means it lets in the heat or cold from outside, which in turn will cause your air conditioner or heater to run more. Also, most building codes require solid-core doors for exterior locations, which includes doors to the garage.

The front door can make a statement about the owners. In the most basic form, a plain, flat panel door is hung in the opening, it's painted, and it's done. A 3'-0" X 6'-8" X 1¾" solid-core, paint-grade door is about $80.00.

At the other end of the spectrum is a fancy, solid-wood door with carved details and glass set into the door, stained a rich, warm color. Both are front doors, but there may be a difference of a thousand dollars or more between the two. Both doors keep the weather, stray animals, and the neighbors' kids out of the house. The difference is aesthetics. How much are you willing to pay for the front door?

(Doors are described by width, height, thickness, material, and finish. Windows also use height and width but eliminate the thickness. Window descriptions add X's and O's. Consider a window in a bedroom. It will have one pane that slides to open and one pane that is stationary. X = movable. O = stationary.)

Room Finish Schedule

Room:	Sq. Ft.	Material	Finish	Color	Mfr.	Model #
North Wall						
South Wall						
East Wall						
West Wall						
Ceiling						
Floor						

Room:	Sq. Ft.	Material	Finish	Color	Mfr.	Model #
North Wall						
South Wall						
East Wall						
West Wall						
Ceiling						
Floor						

Room:	Sq. Ft.	Material	Finish	Color	Mfr.	Model #
North Wall						
South Wall						
East Wall						
West Wall						
Ceiling						
Floor						

Room:	Sq. Ft.	Material	Finish	Color	Mfr.	Model #
North Wall						
South Wall						
East Wall						
West Wall						
Ceiling						
Floor						

Room:	Sq. Ft.	Material	Finish	Color	Mfr.	Model #
North Wall						
South Wall						
East Wall						
West Wall						
Ceiling						
Floor						

Figure 3 Room Finish Schedule

Windows. For older homes in harsh climates, a popular home improvement is to install replacement windows. The upside of replacement windows is that the new windows are dual glazed, which makes them energy efficient. The downside is that some replacement windows allow less light than the windows they replace. (If you live in a hot area such as the southwest desert, a little less light may be good.) This is because they fit inside the existing opening and have a thicker frame. The alternative to replacement windows is to remove the old window, cut the interior and exterior walls to fit the new window, install the new window, and then patch the drywall and stucco or siding. The stucco will show the patched area unless you sandblast the whole house and re-plaster.

Windows and sliding glass doors can be purchased with metal, vinyl, or wood frames. Metal frames are the least expensive and allow more heat transfer than the others. Vinyl and wood frames conduct much less heat; wood has a nicer look and feel but is the most expensive and requires the most maintenance.

The comparable costs of a 4'-0" x 4'-0" window with a horizontal sliding pane (4'-0" x 4'-0" X O) is shown in the following example. The prices were obtained from Dixieline Lumber Company in San Diego. All the windows include *low e*, which is a process that adds a chemical to the glass during manufacture that reduces ultraviolet transmission.

Frame Material	Cost
Wood	$958.00
Vinyl	263.00
Aluminum	223.00

There are a few additional things to know about windows. Most wood frame windows come with an aluminum cladding to protect the wood. In California, all residential windows are dual glazed, meaning that the window has two panes of glass with an air space between the panes. For safety and durability, $1/8$" is the recommended minimum thickness of glass. The airspace reduces the transfer of heat or cold from the outside to the inside. It also acts as a noise barrier.

Cabinets. Cabinetry is an area involving a wide range of prices, because it comes in many styles, materials, grades, and costs. The low end would include cabinets that are picked up at Home Depot and assembled and installed by you, the homeowner. The next step up are cabinets from Home Depot or Lowe's that are factory assembled. A cabinet installer should install them.

At the next level are custom-made cabinets. These cabinets are made to your specifications. Even within this class, there can be a big difference in quality and price. A cabinet could be paint-grade MDF, laminate on particleboard, or solid wood. The faces of drawers and doors could have flat or raised panels. Regardless of what is selected, they are all still cabinets.

In some cases, only custom-made cabinets will work for a particular situation. For years, most bathroom vanities (the cabinets with the sinks) were made with a door under the sink area and no drawer under the sink. If the vanity was wide enough, drawers would be stacked to one side of the vanity. Today, some cabinet makers are designing and building vanities with drawers under the sink. The drawers are U-shaped to fit around the underside of the sink and the plumbing. This is very handy in a bathroom with limited storage space.

Safety

Now let's talk about safety considerations.

Wood vs. metal studs. Many houses are built using wood framing. The most-often-used woods are spruce, pine, fir, and Douglas fir. In California, or in other areas that are subject to earthquakes, Douglas fir should be specified for the framing. Douglas fir is one of the strongest of the woods when it comes to withstanding the stresses placed on a building during an earthquake.

The problem with wood studs is that wood burns. By using metal studs instead of wood studs, you eliminate one fuel source for fires. Metal studs may be called steel studs, but they are made of aluminum. They are as strong as wood studs and don't burn. At Dixieline Lumber in San Diego, metal studs sell for $8.89 each, and wood studs sell for $5.12 each. It is up to you. Is saving three and one-half dollars per stud worth adding more combustible material to your home?

Fire resistance. Wildfires are becoming all too common in California. In 2003, fires consumed hundreds of thousands of acres in Los Angeles, San Bernardino, Riverside, and San Diego Counties. In 2007, Orange County, plus the same four counties as 2003, were burning once again. In the summer of 2008, northern California had over 800 fires, many started by dry lightning strikes. Again in 2017, massive fires burned through parts of California. In 2018, a wildfire wiped out the town of Paradise, California. There have been fires in Arizona and Georgia, as well.

In response to these horrific conflagrations, many of the cities and counties that have been impacted by fires have updated their building codes to make homes more fire resistant. Since the fires of 2007, most San Diego fire departments are requiring that residents clear away dry vegetation from their yards—even in areas that might seem safe from wildfires.

San Diego County offers a 16-point handout titled Fire-Resistive Construction in Wildland Interface Areas. (This

document may be downloaded from
SanDiegoCounty.gov/content/dam/sdc/pds/docs/pds664.pdf.)
San Diego County has become very aggressive in its attempt to
keep the backcountry from going up in flames.

Firebreaks. A firebreak is an area cleared of combustible
materials between a structure and wild lands. Firebreaks are
also called defensible areas. San Diego County mandates at
least 30'- " in all directions. Adjustments are made for smaller
lots. Most other jurisdictions within San Diego County are also
enforcing firebreaks. It is not just areas like Rancho Bernardo
and Jamul that have been hit with wildfires. It is being enforced
in canyon areas throughout the City of San Diego and in La
Mesa.

Fire Sprinklers. For years we have had fire sprinklers in office
and commercial buildings. Now it's time to consider them for
homes in fire-prone areas.

One image of the wildfires of 2007 in San Diego County
still sticks with me. A home in a remote area that was still
standing while everything around it was burnt to a crisp. The
homeowner had installed a sprinkler system on the roof that
sprayed water over the entire roof and exterior of the house.

San Diego County requires fire sprinklers in new
construction and in remodels. A neighbor was required to add

sprinklers not only to the new areas he added to his house but to the existing structure as well.

Roofing. Much of California has outlawed wood shake roofing. The Agoura Fire (Western Los Angeles County and Ventura County) in the 1970s was made worse by the shake roofs in the area. Embers from the fire fell onto the wood roofs and ignited these additional roofs. The best fireproof roofing materials are asphalt shingles and what is known as Bermuda tile. These tiles are a very lightweight concrete that make a nice-looking, fireproof roof.

Mission tile roofs look great but have gaps between the tiles through which embers can enter and ignite the underlying roof structure.

Eaves. Most homes have eaves that extend the roof line past the exterior walls of the building. In most designs, the rafter tails (the ends of the rafters) are exposed, a fire hazard. To remove this fire hazard, the eaves can be enclosed and covered with stucco.

Energy Efficiency

If you are concerned about the indirect costs of the remodel and the ongoing cost of running your home, you should consider the cost of utilities. You can reduce your indirect costs by installing light fixtures that use fluorescent or compact fluorescent lamps. In 2001, the State of California offered rebates to encourage homeowners to replace old windows with energy efficient windows. Go to Energy.gov/eere/femp/energy-incentive-programs-california for the latest information.

In addition, manufacturers of other products will offer rebates from time to time. These rebates may sway you to select one brand over another.

Smart Homes

In today's world of technology, many people are opting for "smart homes." If the technology of smart homes is used a bit aggressively, it may help lower your energy usage. At its most inclusive, a smart home has as much electrical and electronic device connectivity as possible, controlled by the owners' smartphone(s). This could also include Alexa or other similar devices as the focal point. The device converts verbal and/or text commands to electronic signals to control such things as lights, Nest and Ring doorbells, thermostats, and security systems. Even refrigerators, washers, and dryers can be part of your smart home.

Going Green

Going green is not a new fad. Jack in the Box restaurants, for instance, have had energy saving programs since the mid-1980s. The restaurants are designed with energy management systems that control lighting, HVAC, refrigerators, and freezers. Jack in the Box has been using compact fluorescent lamps for a couple decades. McDonald's has experimented with cogeneration of electricity. That is, capturing heat from the kitchen to generate some of its own electricity.

In my opinion, going green, in the context of remodeling your home, means doing as many of the things as possible to reduce energy consumption in the home. In this time of rising fuel prices, going green could save a lot of money over a period of years.

Calculating the return on investment (ROI) for each green system being considered may provide some guidance as to which green systems make sense for the home.

For example, a 13-watt compact fluorescent lamp (CFL) costs about $4.49. This bulb often replaces a 60-watt incandescent bulb. 60 − 13 = 47 watts. A 60-watt incandescent bulb costs about $5.29. The difference is $0.80.

The CFL packaging claims the bulb will pay for itself in less than two years. Since CFLs burn cooler than incandescent bulbs, they are supposed to last many years longer than an incandescent bulb. (Their packaging claims 22-plus years.)

If we say that the light will burn three hours a day, then 3 hours X 47 watts = 141 watts per day; 141 watts per day X 365 days per year = 51.465 KWH (Kilowatt hours) X $0.30 per KWH = $15.44 per year saved by using the CFL lamp, or about

$308.80 over twenty years. The CFL lamp pays for itself in six months or less. This will vary by the cost of electricity where the remodel is located.

Serious about going green? A LEED-certified designer can make that happen for you. LEED, a program put together by the United States Green Building Council,. stands for Leadership in Energy and Environmental Design. When contacting an architect or designer, ask if they are LEED certified. There are a variety of LEED certifications, each of which requires passing an exam. For a residential remodeling project, a designer with a LEED certificate in Homes is best. Short of that, let's look at some green considerations. Two other options are Passive House designers and Energy Star designers. LEED, Passive House, and Energy Star are run by different organizations; they all can help the homeowner reduce energy usage. Do not think that getting an energy-efficient remodel will not be nice. I have seen several LEED buildings that are beautiful.

Photovoltaic Systems

Generating the home's own electricity will require a substantial initial investment, but the payback will be recouped for decades. The most common means to generate your own electricity is by installing photovoltaic (solar) panels on the roof that convert the sun's light to electricity. This type of system can be sized from those that provide some of your electrical needs to systems that generate all the electricity you will need, and then some.

A friend had solar panels installed on his roof about six months ago, here in San Diego County. He mentioned that in the past, in warmer weather they would pay about $300.00 per month for electricity, due to air conditioning usage. At the end of their first six months on solar, San Diego Gas & Electric sent them a check for $42.00. Big difference!

Wind Power

The picture many Americans have of Holland includes a windmill, dikes, and a Dutch girl with wooden shoes. Windmills have been used for pumping water or threshing grain for many centuries. The 21st-century windmill generates electricity.

Wind power for single-family homes is for the person with a lot of land in a remote area. For homes in the middle of a city, it is difficult getting such a system approved by any city planning department. However, the forecast is that one day soon, we will see multi-family developments with small, roof-mounted wind farms.

Solar Water Heating

You can use the sun to heat your water. It is sort of like a huge sun-tea jar. Most solar water heaters are roof-mounted flat panels with piping running through them. The panels concentrate the sun's energy on the piping, which transfers the heat to the water. Solar water heating has been with us since the 1970s.

Tankless Water Heater

A tankless water heater saves money by not keeping a tank of water hot all day and night. A tankless water heater heats the water as it is needed. If you like hot, hot water, have a large household, or don't get a lot of sunny days where you live, a system that combines solar and tankless is an option you might want to consider. The solar system will pre-heat the water; then the tankless heater doesn't have to raise the water temperature as much as if it were working by itself. Be aware that tankless water heaters, including installation, are expensive.

Don't Over-Insulate

Most building departments have a set of minimum insulation requirements for walls, floors, and ceilings. However, putting 6" insulation in a 4"-thick wall will not help. Compressing the insulation counters its usefulness. However, if new exterior walls are being erected as part of the remodel, see if they can be thicker than the existing walls so a thicker insulation may be used.

Over the past several years, many buildings are being wrapped with Dupont Tyvek. This sheet product provides a thermal and moisture barrier that makes the building dryer and more energy efficient.

Consider the Landscaping

Selecting trees and shrubbery for your landscaping is important. First, do not plant eucalyptus trees! Eucalyptus trees are not native to the United States, but rather Australia. Second, they burn very fast and intensely. Third, they are a shallow-root tree, which means they may blow over in a strong wind. Not something to have close to a home!

Energy conservation suggests that you plant deciduous trees near the home to shade it during the summer months and let the sun in during the winter. However, fire codes are changing. In fire-prone areas, trees should not be planted close to structures. This helps keep the fire away from the house. In lieu of trees close to the house, consider retractable patio covers constructed of non-combustible materials.

As much as we like our verdant green lawns, we must face the fact that, at least in California and other areas of the southwest, we have less water available to use. The priority uses of water are cooking, bathing, cleaning, and irrigation for food. Unless you are a farmer, irrigation is the one area that is optional.

Plan your planting to exclude lawn and other thirsty plants. Don't try to grow plants that are native to cool, damp coastal areas in arid and semi-arid locales such as southern California.

A neighbor had a beautiful landscaped yard with very green grass. They removed all the grass and some other thirsty vegetation a couple years ago. They redid their yard to be drought tolerant. They got a nice rebate from the State of California (SaveOurWaterRebates.com/) and the local water agency. It is still the nicest yard on the street.

Install a timer to control all your irrigation and set it for minimum watering times for the planting in each zone. Do not mix plants of different water needs in the same irrigation zone. Drip irrigation systems are considered the most water efficient. Install sprinkler heads so they irrigate planting, not driveways, walkways, and your house.

Find a demonstration garden of plants that grow well in your area with a minimum of water, perhaps at a college or university in your area. Cuyamaca College in Rancho San Diego is one community college with a drought-tolerant demonstration garden and nursery.

Hardscape

Pay attention to the arrangement of the hardscape around your home. Hardscape includes things like driveways, patios, walkways and gravel. Bear in mind that hardscape absorbs heat during the day and then radiates it at the house during the night. The house won't cool down until winter, or it seems that way. Plus, it radiates heat into the atmosphere.

Aging in Place

Not long ago, a retired man (70+), carrying a laundry basket up to the second floor of his home, tripped and fell down the stairs. He sustained a concussion and cuts that required 14 stitches. Two of his doctors found out he lived in a two-story residence and told him to sell and move to a one-story home.

Aging in place, in terms of remodeling, means doing things that will make it easier to function in your home as you age. Examples of this are making all doorways three feet wide so they are wheelchair/walker accessible; or, in the case of the poor fellow who fell down the stairs, having a stairway lift installed.

Other things to consider are barrier-free showers, benches in showers, hand-held shower heads, toilets that are ADA compliant. (Most of them are compliant these days.) While it may be impossible to eliminate all steps from a home, many could be replaced with a ramp.

Having had both knees replaced in the past few years, I can attest to the benefit of all the above improvements. The one item that may need an explanation is a barrier-free shower. This is a shower that has no curb. The bathroom floor flows into the shower floor. The shower floor is sloped slightly steeper than normal to direct the water to the drain. After knee surgery, the shower curb was what seemed the biggest barrier for me for many weeks. Many bathrooms today are designed without a bathtub but with barrier-free showers. Check *Better Homes & Gardens* or Houzz.com for more ideas.

Even if you live in a community with a homeowners' association (HOA,) you should be able to get the needed HOA approval for your aging-in-place projects. Depending on the extent of the work you want done, you may need a building permit as well.

If you decide to do a remodel with aging in place as your primary goal, there are still many selections to make. You will have to pick a tile for the shower floor, at least. Since you are eliminating the curb, you will need a new shower enclosure. Do you want a brushed nickel finish or brass for the trim? Do you want clear or frosted glass? Are you going to change any of the plumbing? As you can see, *decisions, decisions, decisions.*

Nature

The next several sections deal with nature. While we cannot control nature, there are ways we can design our construction to resist the forces of nature. For instance, if you live in a flood-prone area and you want to add a room, figure out a way to elevate the new room so it is higher than a normal first story for your area, above flood stage.

Earthquakes. When considering the design and materials for your remodel, It is important to factor in what natural forces are common in your area. Wood- or metal-stud wall construction is the most tolerant for earthquake-prone areas.

If masonry construction is to be used in a quake prone area, *Do not use unreinforced masonry.* Unreinforced masonry walls are made of red bricks with mortar between the bricks. In an earthquake, these walls will collapse quickly. They may have good strength to hold up roofs and ceilings, but there is nothing to hold them together when the ground starts shaking.

If masonry construction is desired, then use CMUs—concrete masonry units—otherwise known as concrete blocks. The typical size is 8" high by 8" wide by 16" long. Each CMU has two vertical open or hollow areas in the middle, called *cells*.

Masonry construction using concrete blocks starts with rebar, long steel rods, laid in the foundation's footings. About every 4', pieces of rebar with a 90-degree bend are placed in the footing with half the bar horizontal in the footing and the other half (each leg about four feet long) sticking upright. These uprights are positioned to align with the cells in the CMUs. After the footing has been poured, the block wall is started. The first row is mortared to the foundation.

As the wall is erected, the blocks are staggered so that the second row of blocks is one-half block to the right or left of the row below it. The third row matches the first row. The CMUs are adhered to each other with mortar, as are bricks, but there is a big difference. At four-foot-height increments, rebar is inserted vertically into cells every few feet. Also, the top of the blocks at the four-foot increments have a horizontal groove cast into them. Rebar is laid horizontally in this groove. Then concrete is poured into all the cells. The process is repeated for the next four feet. This provides a very strong wall that will withstand a lot of shaking from below and high winds above.

Tornados. Tornados are frightening storm events. In talking with Walter Goodseal of the Urban Design Group in Chula Vista, California, who has designed buildings in many different climate zones, the best shell for a home in tornado prone areas is reinforced masonry construction. According to Goodseal, "Strong walls with good connections will stand up to most tornados, even the roofs. The roofing material may get blown off, but the roof structure and roof deck, assuming good quality materials, should withstand the tornado."

If remodeling in a tornado-prone area, consider reinforced masonry construction for the areas to be remodeled. Windows may get blown out and debris may get blown at the exterior of the building, but after the tornado passes the remodeled area should still be there.

Another key point is having a solid basement that can double as a storm shelter. A concrete-block basement helps with a building-code requirement in most places where tornados occur, and that is the freeze zone. This is the depth to which the ground freezes in winter. In those areas, the foundation must be deeper than the depth of the freeze zone. So why not have a basement?

Since tornados are often associated with lightning, a lightning rod is not a bad investment either.

Snow. The main problem with snow is its weight. In a heavy snowstorm, the snow will build up on the roof. As more snow falls, the weight on the roof gets heavier and heavier. If the roof's structure is not strong enough, the roof may no longer be able to hold the weight and will collapse. This could weaken the frame of the building. If the storm was accompanied by strong winds that cause snow drifts, the weight of the snow on the drift side of the home could also fail.

Once again, masonry construction is recommended to prevent this possibility. Also, it is best to double-up joists or rafters, depending on the roof design. Doubling up means to use two boards nailed or screwed together instead of the normal single board. (A joist is a single board, such as a 2" x 12", that spans from one wall to another and is flat. Joists are installed on edge, meaning its 12" dimension is vertical. A rafter is like a joist except that it is installed on an angle for a pitched roof.)

Stucco or plaster is not a good exterior finish in snowy areas. Snow is frozen water. As temperatures warm and the snow against the home melts, some of that moisture gets into the stucco. Stucco is applied to a metal lath that covers the wall framing. As the snow melts, some of the moisture gets to the lath. Over time the lath can rust and fail, causing it and the stucco to erode.

One partial solution is to design the exterior walls with a wainscot (pronounced *Wayne's coat*.) A wainscot is an area about four feet high from the ground or floor up, that runs the length of a wall. In this situation, a wainscot will have a brick or wood veneer on it for aesthetics. Having a wainscot will keep the moisture from ruining the stucco, but only for the height of the stucco covered by the wainscot.

Rain and Flooding. Hurricanes are different from tornados. Hurricanes have lots of rain and wind, and for a period of days, whereas tornados form, peak, and dissipate in a matter of hours. In 2017, hurricanes damaged much larger areas than tornados did.

A hurricane's wind can have a devastating impact on the areas it hits. Reinforced masonry construction can prevent a lot of damage to a home. Couple it with good lumber and strong connections, and such a building can withstand a lot of what a hurricane dishes out.

Hurricanes dump a lot of rain as they pass through an area. In many cases, there will be flooding in the aftermath of a hurricane, such as Hurricane Harvey, which hit Houston, Texas, in 2017. Along the Atlantic and Gulf of Mexico coastlines, storm surge can be very damaging.

To protect a home from these forces, the home must have a raised foundation to keep the living area above the water. Along the Gulf Coast in Florida, you will see homes built with a carport at ground level and the living area on the second floor. Reinforced masonry construction with deep footings is key.

Materials

The ordering and handling of materials can impact the pace of a project in both new and remodel projects.

Ordering Materials. As discussed above, a lot of different materials go into a home, such as doors, windows, roofing, and water heaters. Materials that will be hidden from view when the job is done, such as studs, should be left to the contractor to order.

For those items that will be visible when the project is done, such as doors, flooring, and tile, you, the homeowner, may want to order them or accompany the contractor to select them. With each item, be sure to ask what the return policy is;

many special orders are non-returnable. Some material suppliers charge a restocking fee for returned items.

A national tile distributer will take back any tile that is their product. Anything that they say is from an outside source, they will not take back, whether you want to return some or all of that tile. Nowhere on their order and invoice forms is this policy mentioned. So, *beware!*

Also, double-check, even triple-check, the dimensions of the things you order. If you order the wrong size, the wrong finish, or the wrong color, you may be unable to return it.

Lead Time. Consider each item's lead-time. How much time will pass from the time it is ordered until it is delivered to the local supplier or to the job?

For example, Velux skylights take about a week in Southern California. Some fireplace doors can take up to 12 weeks. Some of the fancy doors mentioned earlier in this chapter can take three to four months. How does the lead-time for each item fit into your job schedule?

As you can see, a remodel has a lot of variables, and these can differ from one geographic area of the country to the next. The one weather element most areas of the country get is wind, but that varies in intensity. It all comes down to what is needed, when will it arrive, and what is affordable.

When to Order. A lot of materials go into a remodel, too, as you can tell from the various topics in this chapter. Whether materials are being ordered by the you or the contractor, purchase or order the materials as soon as possible, especially if they are things that will be visible after the job is complete.

Why, you ask?

The answer is shipping.

Over the past three years I have had to return three refrigerators, a door, and a roll of vinyl flooring because they were all damaged in shipping. The refrigerators had scratches on the doors and side. The roll of flooring looked like it had been driven over a few times between the factory and our home. The door had a big gouge in one corner.

All these products had been packaged at the factory with what looked like adequate protection. It appears that once they left their factories, caution—and the products—were thrown to the wind by the people who handled the products until they arrived at our home.

Besides the damage that may occur in transit, the transit itself can be a problem. A friend ordered two doors. He was told they would be ready for pickup in two weeks. At the two-week mark, they were in transit somewhere in Kansas. At the four-week mark, they were still in transit somewhere in Kansas. It can't be that difficult to get out of Kansas! The doors had glass insets. When the doors did arrive, several of the glass insets were broken.

Order early so there is time for the materials to get to you in time and the job is not held up while waiting for the "missing" materials. Also, if some item is damaged in transit, it must be returned, and a replacement must be ordered. More waiting time.

Stucco. In the West, many houses have a stucco (plaster) exterior. When it comes time to remodel, there is a good chance that some of the existing stucco will have to be patched or new walls have been added that will need stucco. The existing stucco and the new stucco will never match. The reason is that the finish coat of stucco, called the color coat, is applied by hand. Each plasterer has a unique signature to his trowel strokes, sort of a fingerprint. Even the best of plasterers are going to have a hard time matching someone else's trowel stroke. To get all the stucco on a house to match after the remodel, the existing stucco should be sandblasted and then re-plastered. A less effective method is to power-wash the existing stucco and then apply a very light color coat.

Power washing uses water under moderate pressure, like a fire hose, to wash the old stucco. In most cases, power washing does a fair job. Where it fails is on areas that get very little sunlight and at the line where the old and new stucco meet. In both cases, it is easy to pick out these transitions after the color coat is applied.

On the other hand, sandblasting uses sand under high pressure to remove the stucco color-coat on the existing portion of the house. Then the entire house is color-coated, and it all looks the same, terrific.

If your stucco has been painted, new stucco won't adhere as well to paint as to stucco. Therefore, you would want to sandblast or power-wash the existing stucco before another coat is applied. Either method is preferable to doing nothing.

You can't build a great building on a weak foundation.

—Gordon B. Hinckley

Chapter 7. Picking a Contractor

Up to this point, you have decided to remodel your house. You have had construction documents prepared, picked the materials, and have the money. It's time to pick a contractor.

The biggest question on many people's minds after "How much will it cost?" is "How do I pick a good contractor?" The California State Contractors License Board has ten suggestions.

1. Hire only licensed contractors.
2. Check the contractor's license number.
3. Get three references and review past work.
4. Get at least three bids.
5. Get a written contract and do not sign anything until you completely understand the terms.

6. Pay 10% down or $1,000.00, whichever is less.

7. Don't let payments get ahead of work. Keep records of payments.

8. Don't make final payment until you're satisfied with the job.

9. Don't pay cash.

10. Keep a job file of all the papers relating to the project.[9]

CAL California has strict regulations covering construction contractors. Many other states exert little or no control over these same businesses. For instance, Louisiana seems to be less concerned with regulating contractors and construction than it is with the crawfish industry. This may have changed since Hurricane Katrina. Most states are in the middle, with limited to moderate licensing or regulation over the construction trades.

Your cousin Fred is a contractor. Piece of cake, right? WRONG! Your cousin Fred is the next-to-last person you should use. Odds are, because he is your cousin, the two of you are going to have a hard time establishing a proper business relationship. The same goes for friends who are contractors.

---

[9] California Contractors State License Board, *What You Should Know Before You Hire a Contractor* (Sacramento, CA: California Contractors State License Board, 1999).

Never, *never* hire a general contractor who happens to be in the neighborhood and approaches you. This is the last person you should use. This is a sign of a scam artist or con man. In his book *How to Hire a Home Improvement Contractor Without Getting Chiseled*, Tom Philbin relates horror story after horror story of people being ripped off by contractors who just show up at the door. Even though the book is now several years old, it is worth reading.

Also, forget the telephone book, if you even have one anymore. Be a bit leery of contractors who pop up in Google searches. Word of mouth or recommendations from others who have done a remodel in the recent past are the best. The architect you use should have a list of contractors the architect is comfortable recommending. If you can't come up with 12 contractors, try calling the BIA, the Building Industry Association (BIAsandiego.org; BIA websites are local), the Associated Builders and Contractors (ABC, ABC.org), and the Associated General Contractors of America (AGCA, AGC.org). The members of these organizations have one leg up on someone from a Google search, because the members tend to be committed to the community, are interested in improving their operations, and have established businesses.

Don't feel that you must sign a contract with a particular contractor. Anyone who uses high-pressure tactics to encourage or force you to sign with them should raise warning flags immediately! This is a prime tactic of scam artists. As we will see later, when we talk about the bidding process, it takes time to put a solid proposal together. The contractor, in turn, should give you a reasonable amount of time to review the bids.

Compiling a List of Contractors

The first step is to gather the names of general contractors. The best way to compile the list of contractors who will be considered for the remodel is to ask people you trust. Ask the architect you used for your plans. Ask neighbors and friends who have had remodels completed in the past two years about the contractor they used. Ask people you know at work, at school, at your place of worship, and at other places you frequent. My goal would be to collect the names of about 12 general contractors. Why so many? The answer is simple. We want to weed through the list and eliminate some of them.

Let's say that a list of 12 contractors has been compiled, without Google. How do we cut down the list? And why do we want to? You want to cut down the list to eliminate any contractor who is a scam artist or con man. You want to get rid of any contractor who is less than honest, less than professional, a poor businessperson, or unreliable.

How do you pick a general contractor from your list? How do you accomplish this pruning of the list?

In our society, we have a penchant for trying to get a deal on everything. Buying based on price alone can be a very bad idea for such complicated things as remodeling your house. For major investments, try to find a happy median point that takes into consideration such things as price, quality, features, and comfort.

For most of us, our home is the biggest investment we will ever make. That is even truer in California's major metropolitan areas. It makes sense to protect that investment.

Another place to find remodeling contractors is the National Association for the Remodeling Industry (NARI.org/).

Types of Contractors

There are two types of contractors: general and specialty. A general contractor will be the contractor in charge of a remodel. Specialty contractors specialize in a trade such as plumbing or tile setting. Unless you are acting as owner-builder, you will hire a general contractor. The general contractor will use in-house employees, subcontractors, or a combination of employees and subcontractors to perform the work on the remodel.

In some states, the general contractor may be called a home improvement contractor or a remodeling contractor. In California, a home improvement certificate must be added to any contractor's license for that contractor to be eligible to work on any residential property, and the State of California considers anything done to a residence to be a home improvement project.

We'll assume that for the purposes of this book that we are dealing with general contractors. You have compiled a list of, say, 12 contractors. When you make the initial call to a contractor on the list, the two of you are at cross purposes. The contractor is in sales mode. You are trying to get a feel for the contractor. Do you feel you can and want to do business with them? It is suggested that you download a copy of the First Contact with Contractor form (see Figure 4) for each contractor you call. *(This worksheet, as well as other worksheets and checklists, is available in full-size format at no cost, from PeterAKlein.com.)*

Here are the things you want to accomplish:

- Introduce yourself and explain what you are planning to do. Be brief.
- Tell the contractor where you got his or her name.
- Ask if they are licensed or registered (depending on locale).
- Ask if they can take on new work.
- Ask if they have experience in similar projects.
- See if you feel okay with each other over the phone.

- Set up a time to have a preliminary meeting, at the remodel location.

- Give the contractor a list of things to bring to the meeting.

Beyond the items listed in Figure 4 First Contact with Contractor, you want the contractors to bring you the tools to help you keep them on your list or eliminate them from your list.

Never accept a bid from a contractor who has not looked at your plans nor visited the job site and gives you the bid over the phone. How in the world can they give you an accurate bid without knowing see your plans?

New Projects

If the contractor can't take on any new projects at the current time, this company is not out of the running. Honesty is one of the things you are trying to find. You don't want a contractor who has more work than they can handle. If you are not in a rush, which you shouldn't be, this contractor might be a good prospect.

If you are not in a rush and feel good about the contractor, find out when the contractor could be available. If the contractor can't get to new work for more than six months, it is best to thank them and scratch them off the list. Otherwise, set up a meeting with the contractor as you would anyone else on the list.

First Contact with Contractor

Copyright 2020 by Peter A. Klein, all rights reserved.

Name of Business: _____

Telephone Number: _____

Contact Person: _____

Title: _____

Salesperson Registration Number: _____

Do you feel comfortable this person over the phone? _____

Briefly explain what you planning to do.

Tell the contractor where you got their name.

Is the contractor currently licensed by the State/City? Yes / No / Not required

Is the contractor experienced in projects similar to what I want to do? Yes / No

Can you take on new work at this time?   Yes / No

Set up a time to have a preliminary meeting, at the remodel location.

Date: _____ at Time: _____

Ask the contractor to bring the following things with them when they meet with you:

   1. Wallet card or photocopy of contractor's license; home improvement certificate, if required in your locale.

   2. Insurance certificates for workers' compensation, liability vehicle liability and contractor's bond if required

   3. A list of references, both good and not so good

Notes:

Figure 4 First Contact with Contractor

Experienced in Similar Projects

If you are planning to have a swimming pool built in your back yard, you are not going to call a drywall contractor. If you want to add a room to your house you would call a general contractor who specializes in residential work. You want to call a general contractor who has experience with projects like what you want to do. A contractor who specializes in what are called "tenant improvements" (TIs) may not be a good match for a residential room addition. (A tenant improvement is construction that improves the spaces of a tenant in a commercial building.) There are some contractors who do both residential and commercial projects quite well. Check out their residential remodel history.

After you have called all the contractors on your list, you may have already eliminated some of them. For those who made the cut, set up an appointment for them to meet you at the site of the remodel. This gives both sides a chance to continue sizing up each other.

Your Tools

During your initial contact with a contractor, you want the contractor to provide you with certain information. This information will be used to try to disqualify the contractor. Ask the contractor to bring the following items to the initial meeting:

- If general contractors or home improvement contractors must be registered or licensed in your state, you want to see each contractor's registration certificate or license.

- If your state requires an additional certificate for home improvement work, you want to see that as well.

- Insurance certificates for workers compensation insurance, liability insurance, contractor's bond, if required by the state, and vehicle liability insurance.

- A list of references, both good and bad.

You want the contractors to bring photocopies of the paperwork mentioned above. After meeting each contractor, it is time for you to go to work. The information provided by each contractor will now be verified for correctness. For each contractor, make a copy of the Contractor Checklist (see Figure 5. *(This checklist, as well as other worksheets and checklists, is available in full-size format at no cost, from PeterAKlein.com.)*

Is the Contractor Licensed?

Forty-three states and the District of Columbia have some mechanism for regulating contractors. The National Association of State Contractors Licensing Agencies can provide you with a current list.

Twelve states require that all trades be licensed. These states are Alaska, Arizona, Arkansas, California, Florida, Kentucky,

Contractor Checklist

Business Name: _____

Contractor's Name: _____

Salesperson's Name: _____

Contractor's Address: _____

City, State Zip: _____

Phone: _____ Cell: _____ email: _____

Contractor's License Number: _____ Is the license valid? Yes / No

Salesperson Registration Number: _____ Is the license valid? Yes / No

Liability Insurance -   Carrier_____ Policy # _____

Workers Compensation – Carrier: _____ Policy # _____

Vehicle Liability –   Carrier: _____ Policy # _____

Contractor's Bond –   Carrier: _____ Policy # _____

Better Business Bureau –   any complaints? _____

State Contractor's License Board – any complaints? _____

Does the contractor have experience in the type of planned project?   Yes / No

How many years in business? _____   _   How many current jobs? _____

Who will run my job? _____

Which trades will be done in-house? _____

What is the contractor's credit rating? (1 is poor and 5 is great)   1   2   3   4   5

References (Suppliers, Subcontractors & Customers):

Figure 5 Contractor Checklist

Nevada, New Mexico, Oregon, South Carolina, Tennessee, and Utah.

Seven states have no requirements or qualifications for any type of contractor. They are Iowa, Kansas, Louisiana, Nebraska, New York, Rhode Island, and Washington. In New York, local governments may require contractors to obtain city licenses. This is the case in New York City. In fact, New York City has a licensing process much like California and Nevada.

The rest of the states require that certain specialty contractors be licensed. The requirements cover contractors working in the electrical, plumbing, and mechanical trades.

Some states have reciprocity for licensees. For example, a contractor licensed in Nevada may obtain a California license of the same type without going through the examination process because the licensing requirements are very similar in the two states. An electrical contractor licensed in North Carolina has reciprocity in Alabama, Florida, Mississippi, South Carolina, Virginia, and West Virginia.

Check with your local building department to find out what is required in your area. Be wary if you live in an area that does not regulate contractors.

There are two sites on the Internet where each state's licensing requirements may be verified: HomeAdvisor or your state's website.

At HomeAdvisor you can select your state and find the licensing requirements for the state; go to HomeAdvisor.com/r/state-by-state-licensing-requirements/. Then click on your state. If licensing is required, go to the appropriate entity's website.

To visit your state's website, search for State.XX.us, where *XX* (not case sensitive) is the two-character postal abbreviation of your state. New Jersey would be State.nj.us. Once you have the state's website displayed on your computer's screen, you must then find the proper agency. In California, you want the State Contractors License Board. In other states, start with the Secretary of State's office or do a search for Occupational and Professional Licensing, Occupational and Professional Registration, Professional and Occupational Licensing, or Professional and Occupational Registration.

While you are looking at your state's website, go to the Attorney General's website, the consumer affairs or consumer protection web page(s.) Even states with limited or no contractor licensing requirements have web pages devoted to explaining how to hire a residential contractor.

Verifying the License

If contractor licensing or registration is required where you live, verify that the licenses of the contractors on your list are valid. Contact the licensing agency for your state or locale.

The licensing agency may also be able to tell you if any of the contractors have any complaints filed against them. If there is no requirement for general contractors to be licensed, check with your state or local consumer protection agency to see if any complaints have been filed against any of the contractors on your list.

CAL   Verifying A Contractor's License in California

Contracting without a license is illegal in California, if the amount of the contract is over $500.00. You're not going to get much of a remodel for $500.00. Immediately eliminate a contractor from consideration if they do not have a valid contractor's license. Using an unlicensed contractor is one of the most foolish things you can do. By using an unlicensed contractor, you forfeit any remedies you will have if anything goes wrong. An unlicensed contractor is much more likely to take advantage of you than a licensed contractor. The Contractors State License Board is the state agency that regulates contractors in California.

Contact the Contractors State License Board to verify that the contractors you are screening are licensed. You have two goals here.

The first is to verify each contractor's license. The second is to get a feel for the contractor.

If a license number you are checking turns out to be invalid, that contractor falls off the list. (If a contractor on your list turns out to be unlicensed, report the situation to the Contractors State License Board.)

The toll-free telephone number is 800-321-CSLB (2752). The Contractors State License Board website address is CSLB.ca.gov/.

To find out if any complaints have been filed against a contractor, you will need to call the Contractors State License Board.

Another source of information about complaints is the Better Business Bureau. Better Business Bureaus in most large cities have websites you can check, or you may call them on the telephone. Joining the Better Business Bureau costs money. Many businesses would rather put that money into other things, so not belonging is not a disqualifier.

A complaint is not an automatic disqualification. A contractor that does many jobs each year and has been in business for several years is bound to have had a complaint or two. If the complaints were ignored, that company falls off your list. If the contractor made reasonable efforts to resolve the complaints, that company may be worth keeping on your list. Ask the contractor about it.

Liability Insurance

Does the contractor have liability insurance? If not, that company falls off your list. The liability insurance protects you if the contractor is negligent in constructing your remodel. In the wake of September 11, the cost of insurance for businesses has skyrocketed. Increases of 50% to 200% are common, compared to previous years. However, it is a cost of doing business and is something a contractor must have.

What is the limit of each contractor's liability insurance? Is it sufficient to cover the costs of making your home right if something goes wrong? Talk to your insurance agent to see what is best for your circumstances. $1,000,000.00 is the common minimum coverage a general contractor should carry.

Contractor's Bond

Several states, including California, require contractors to carry a contractor bond, or surety bond. The bond is like a security deposit with the state. The insurance company that issues the bond would have to pay the state if the contractor was convicted of violating certain provisions of the contractor license laws.

Worker's Compensation Insurance

Construction is a very dangerous business. There aren't many trade people who are approaching retirement age who don't have bad knees, bad backs, or both. Lime in plaster bleaches the skin of most plasterers. An unknown number of nails have gone through my boots. Hammers have hit my fingers. One time I fell backwards while carrying a beam, which bruised a bunch of ribs. Friends have nailed toes to roofs, been electrocuted, cut off fingers with saws, and taken two- and three-story falls.

This is not meant to scare you, but to let you know how important it is for a contractor to have worker's compensation insurance.

CAL   In California many contractors get their coverage from the State Workers Compensation Fund. Some larger contractors may be self-insured.

Vehicle Liability Insurance

This is an item many people don't ask to see. The contractor's vehicle liability insurance should cover all employees of the company while on company business. The coverage should include the vehicles owned by the contractor, as well as employee-owned vehicles used for company business.

A quick summary would show us that when we interview a contractor, the contractor should provide us with a copy of their contractor's license, registration, and/or home improvement license, if required in your area. They should also provide evidence of liability insurance, worker's compensation coverage, vehicle liability insurance, and contractor's bond, if required. The insurance certificate will have the name of the agent on it. Call and verify that the insurance is in force. Insurance agents who work with contractors are used to these calls. If any of the policies or bonds is not enforce, that contractor is off your list.

References

Not every job is going to sail along smoothly. See if you can find out how the contractors handle those adverse situations. This is where the contractor's references come into play. Work the references. To start your weeding-out process, drive by several of the jobs listed by each contractor.

Also, ask for a reference for a job that didn't go that well; one that is not on the contractor's references list. The reason you want this information is find out how the contractors handle the mistakes, disagreements with owners, and other adverse situations. If they give you the name of a homeowner whose job had problems, you can call this person to see if the contractor followed up and rectified the problem or problems. You can also see if the follow-up was done soon after the contractor was contacted.

Next, ask each contractor to call three homeowners you have picked from their lists. Have the contractor ask the homeowners for permission for you to call them. You want to talk to these previous clients without the contractor's being around, and you want to visit these jobs to see if you want this company working for you. For this task, make a copy of the Review of Contractor's Past Job (see Figure 6; *this worksheet, as well as other worksheets and checklists, is available in full-size format at no cost, from PeterAKlein.com.*)

When you call the homeowners, be polite and courteous. They are doing you a big favor. The goal of the call is to set up an appointment for you to walk through the remodeled area of their homes. You are imposing on them, but they are often glad to show off their pride and joy. If they aren't, try to find out why. If a previous client will talk to you but won't agree to your visiting their home, get as much information from them as possible. Call the contractor to set up contact with another of their previous clients for you to visit.

Always thank the previous clients!

Visiting Previous Jobs

When you visit jobs from a reference list, be on time. Be polite and courteous. Ask if you can open doors and drawers of cabinetry that were part of the project. Ask the owner if they are pleased with the outcome of the project. What problems, if any, were encountered during construction? How did the contractor handle these problems? Was the job kept neat and clean? Would the homeowner use the contractor again? What percentage over or under the contract price did the job cost at completion? What was the cause of the biggest change order, if there were any? Use the Review of Contractor's Past Job (Figure 6) for these job visits.

If you have weeded out any contractors after talking to previous customers and visiting some of these previous jobs, do the contractor the courtesy of calling to let them know they are no longer in contention. If they ask why, tell them.

For those contractors still in the running, your next request is to visit a current job, when the homeowner is home. Go through the same process as you did when visiting the completed jobs.

The Contractor's Office

It is a good idea to visit the contractor's place of business. The idea here is to verify that the contractor has some roots in the area. You want to make sure the contractor is not doing business out of the back of a pickup truck and can make a quick get-away. What do you do if the contractor's business address is a post office box, or a letter drop in a FedEx store; is this a screen to prevent you from tracing them?

If the contractor works out or their home that is alright, if they own the home. If they are renting and have been at the present address for several years, they would seem stable. An apartment indicates less stability in their lives, unless they own

Checklist for Past Jobs

Owner Name: _____ Phone: _____

Job Address: _____

City, State Zip: _____

Is the owner pleased with the outcome of the project?   Yes / No

What problems, if any, were encountered during construction? _____

How did the contractor handle these problems?_____

Was the job kept neat and clean?   Yes / No

Would the homeowner use the contractor again?   Yes / No

If No, why not? _____

What percentage over or under the contract price did the job cost at completion? _____%

What was the cause of the biggest change order(s)? _____

How long ago was the job completed? _____

How does the remodeled area look for its age? _____

Are the walls square and plumb? _____

Is the wall texture even and consistent inside and out? _____

Can you see nail and tape lines in the drywall? _____

Are the corners and joints of trim, moldings, and casings tight, smooth and flush? _____

Do cabinets fit snuggly together? Are drawers and doors square and level? _____

What did you see that you really liked? _____

What did you see that you really didn't like? _____

Were there any problems financially? Did the contractor pay his bills on time? _____

Figure 6 Review of Contractor's Past Job

the apartment building. Along with the other qualifications we have discussed, you are looking for a contractor who has been in business for a few years, who has roots in the community, and who isn't a flight risk.

The Bidding Process

For the contractors who haven't fallen by the wayside, it is time for them to go to work. You should get at least three written proposals or bids. More than that is better. To get the written proposals from your list of contractors, you will need a several sets of construction documents for each contractor. They will need one set for themselves and others for their subcontractors to use.

Track the number of sets of construction documents that have been checked out to each contractor. Get the sets back from all contractors. Reissue then to the contractor you select. You may want to number each set of construction documents before handing out for bidding, so you can track which set went to which contractor. Download the Construction Document Checkout List (see Figure 7) to keep track of the sets. *(This worksheet, as well as other worksheets and checklists, is available in full-size format at no cost, from PeterAKlein.com.)*

Peter A. Klein

Contractor		Date Out	Set Numbers	Date Returned	Bid Due Date

Figure 7 Construction Document Checkout List

One thing that should make a contractor spend a little more time going over your construction documents, so as not to not miss anything, is for you to require that the contractors must initial each page of the construction documents during the estimating. This only ensures that the construction documents were opened to each page while they were in the contractor's possession.

However, initialing each page closes an escape route for the contractor because they cannot claim they did not see an item. Their initials indicate that they looked at the page on which an item was shown or noted.

On many large residential projects and on most commercial projects, the specifications are contained on a separate book, often an 8½" by 11" report cover or binder. If you have a large enough project to have its own specification book, require the contractors to initial each page of the specifications as well as the plans. Many are now on CD-ROMs, which eliminates the possibility of having each page initialed.

Some contractors use computer programs to prepare their proposals. Three of these programs are Means, Timberline, and Exactimate. Ask the contractors you have invited to bid on your project if they use any software for preparing bids. If they do, ask for a copy of their printout for your project. If they are willing to share this with you, they would seem to be above board.

Sharing the printout will do two things. First, it will give you an idea of how much detail they put into the bid. Second, it will give you an idea of the materials and labor involved in your project. Contractors who use software to help with the estimating process will be more consistent with their bids and have fewer computational mistakes. Using a computer in bid preparation is not a guarantee that the estimator didn't miss something, but it is an indicator that the contractor is trying to be a good businessperson.

Contractor David Rawls uses the estimating program Exactimate. He enters the information into the software about the size of the rooms that will be involved by the project, data for the trades he performs in-house, and the proposals from his subcontractors. After all the data has been entered, he prints the report and gives it to the customer as his bid. This is a nice touch. It shows the homeowner where their money is being spent and that everything is out in the open.

The Pre-Bid Meeting

Here is a tactic that may help you eliminate one or more of the contractors from your list: have a pre-bid meeting. This is a helpful technique to use if you are pressed for time. To pull this off takes a bit of nerve. Pick a date and time, 10 to 14 days out. Call each of the contractors who are still on your list. Tell them that you are ready for them to bid the project. Then tell them that the only time you have available is the date and time you selected. (You can throw in a comment about your hectic schedule if you want.) If the contractor is free at that time, they will be there. If you want to be up front, tell the contractors that your time is very limited, and you are having a pre-bid group meeting of contractors under serious consideration. Some will decline immediately. Those that decline are off the list.

When all the contractors have arrived, you walk the job and discuss the plans with the group. If one asks a question, they all get the answer. Bidding is on a more level playing field.

This tactic will eliminate any contractors who don't like competitive bidding. I did this when I wanted to repaint my house several years ago. One guy drove up, saw the other trucks and drove off. If a contractor doesn't like the competition, it is a good idea for that company to be removed from your list. Competitive bidding is a part of the contracting business.

As the contractors arrive, give each at least two sets of the construction documents. Keep a list of how many sets of construction documents each contractor has, when they went out, and when they came back. Ask each contractor how long it will take for them to work up an estimate. Write that down. Be prepared to wait.

As the bids come in, get the plans back from the contractors. When you sign the contract with one of the contractors, you will have several plans available for the actual construction. Be sure to keep a couple of sets for yourself.

Now is a good time to reflect back on the behavior of the contractors whom you have asked to bid on your remodel. Have any of them been slow to provide the information you have requested? Have any of them given you excuses for being late, missing documents, and so on? This may be their modus operandi. You may want to consider eliminating these contractors.

How Bidding Works

If your project involves 10 trades, there will be at least 10 material take-offs that must be done, for each general contractor and the associated subcontractors. A material take-off is a time-consuming task. If we use carpentry as our example, the contractor must measure each wall that must be built, any floors and ceilings, and the roof.

For each wall, the contractor must determine the number of studs and their height, the bottom plate, the top plates, shear paneling, any headers, and any required structural hardware. The bottom plate is the board that is the bottom of the wall. One top plate holds the studs in position. The other is used to tie walls together at corners. The studs are the vertical members of the wall. Headers are heavier boards that carry the roof load over doors and windows. Shear panels are sheets of plywood that are nailed to the outside of exterior walls to provide seismic strength. Structural hardware includes things like joist hangers.

This process is repeated for each wall, the floor, ceiling, and roof. The contractor must figure in some waste as well.

The contractor will generate a lumber list from the take-off. From the lumber list, he can get a bid for the lumber, nails, and structural hardware. While the lumberyard is pricing the lumber list, the framing contractor will calculate the labor needed to build your remodel. Overhead and profit are then added.

Each trade performs a similar process. When completed, each subcontractor sends their proposal to the general contractor. The general contractor adds in things like portable toilets, dumpsters, and cleanup. They will add overhead and profit. This all takes time.

Some of the subcontractors may want to visit your house before preparing their bids for the general contractor. This is especially true if you are including work in parts of the home that are not part of the remodel, such as repainting the interior of the rest of your house. The painting contractor will want to see the condition of the existing walls. If a piece of special equipment is needed for your job, the subcontractor who will be using the equipment may want to come by and see if they can get the equipment where they need it.

Bids should include a description of the work to be performed. If the language in the proposal strikes you as being too vague or not accurately describing the work, the materials, or some other aspect of the job, ask that the bid be rewritten. Tell the contractor why you want it rewritten. Since the contractor will use the same language in the contract, you want the bid to be very accurate, detailed, and descriptive.

Never accept a bid that is not in writing. Verbal contracts are legal. However, if you and the contractor wind up in arbitration or in court, a written contract gives the arbitrator or the court a document on which to base their decision. If the contract is not in writing, either party can have memory lapses. You want to be able to look it up.

Reviewing the Bids

The proposals should be dated, signed, and good for 30 days or longer. If a contractor tells you that the bid is good for a very limited time, less than two weeks, show them the door. This is a technique used by con men and scam artists.

Contracting is not like selling beef or buffalo meat door-to-door. How many of you have been approached by the driver of a yellowish truck with a swan on the side? His opening line is always, "I was in the neighborhood and had half a hippo left over and wanted to see if you wanted it for a real good deal." It's a scam. They may have been in the neighborhood to make a delivery to someone who ordered a freezer's worth of moose meat, but he's a door-to-door salesman. Most contractors look for more effective ways to market their companies.

Be suspicious of bids that come at even dollar amounts. Walter Goodseal of the Urban Design Group designs a wide variety of buildings, but he also puts together construction estimates for his design projects, so he can help his clients figure out what their project will cost before they get a contractor's bid. He feels that a bid of say $150,000.00 or $400,000.00 is not be trusted.

A contractor who has put together a good proposal will submit a more precise number, like $154,231.25. The number may be rounded a little to eliminate the twenty-five cents, but will not a such an even number; $154,231.00 is okay, but $150,000.00 is not.

Your designer should have been able to provide a design that covers your needs but was also able to design something that would give you an idea of what the general contractors' bids will be.

Construction is not perishable. You do not need to sign on the dotted line today or the lumber spoils. At the time this book was written, we were not in a period with a fluctuating market for building materials. In those times, the fluctuations seem to affect one or two trades or materials, but not the whole project. If the market for some material is fluctuating a lot, most contractors you talk to will tell you about the market for that material. That is the time a bid may good for two weeks or less. In that situation, the portion of the bid that doesn't involve the volatile material should be good for 30 days.

In March 2002, President George H. W. Bush imposed a 29% tariff on Canadian lumber. Most of this lumber is soft wood used in construction outside of California. The primary wood used in California is Douglas fir, a hardwood. This tariff drove up the cost of residential construction in California, until the nervousness wore off.

Who Do You Select?

You have received several bids. Which contractor do you select? For a moment, assume that all other qualifications are equal. Many consumer advocates, contracting folklore, and my own experience suggest you throw out the lowest bid—the one that is significantly lower than the rest of the proposals you received. A bid that far below the rest means that the contractor either doesn't know how to estimate or missed something or both.

The highest bid should be viewed with skepticism as well. Again, we are talking about a proposal that is much higher than the next highest proposal you have received. A proposal this high can mean the contractor either didn't want the job or is trying make a fast buck at your expense.

In the ideal setting, you will have more than one bid in the middle. The closer together they are, the better. They validate each other. Since we don't live in an ideal world, you will have to look at other factors to help you make your decision. By the time you have gotten to this stage, most of the contractors on your short list should be on the up and up.

How do you feel about working with each of these individuals and their companies? How many years they have been in business? How many years have they been in construction? How many projects like yours have they done? Who will be running your job?

Almost every contractor started out working in a trade. Many general contractors were carpenters. After mastering carpentry, they would run a carpentry crew. Next, they might have worked as a superintendent for a builder. The experience they gained gave them the knowledge to start their own contracting business.

Carpenters interact with more workers from other trades than just about any other specialty in construction. Carpenters learn how to adjust the construction if the foundation is out of square. They are asked to place extra lumber in key places so that other trades can attach things like cabinets, lighting, and ducting to walls and ceilings.

If you have diligently followed the ideas we've discussed so far, you have done as much as possible to eliminate the so-so contractors and the con men. They don't want to work as hard as you have made them work to get to this point. From the time you called your first contractor until you have received all the bids, two months or more could have passed. That is too long for a con man. They want to be in and out of an area in a few weeks.

If you are having a difficult time deciding which contractor to use, you can make one more check. Check out the contractors' finances. Run a Dunn and Bradstreet (D&B) report on one or more of the contractors on your short list. Have your bank do it or go to DNB.com/ or call 844-238-4939.

Be patient. From start to finish, remodeling your home can be a long process if you want it done right. In my years of managing projects, the projects that had the best results were the ones that had the most effort invested in planning. Plan, plan, plan!

He builded better than he knew; The conscious stone to beauty grew.

—Emerson, *The Prophet*

Chapter 8. The Construction

The design is set, the permits are in hand, a contractor has been selected, and a contract is signed. Now the work is about to begin! This chapter describes what to expect during the actual construction. More decisions await. The first decision is whether to stay or move out temporarily.

Stay or Move

Questions to ask: Is the area that is being remodeled far enough away from the main areas of your house that you will not be uprooted by the construction? Are you early risers? Do you thrive on turmoil? If you answered yes to these questions, you should be able stay at home during the remodel.

If turmoil drives you crazy, if the work will be very extensive, affecting much of your house, you may want to pack up and go to a hotel or apartment. That will add to the cost of doing the project. An additional thing to consider is whether you want or need to pack up some or all your belongings.

During a remodel at my house, we had about half our belongings in half the garage and new materials in the other half. I am one of those people who feels if you have a two-car garage and two cars, both cars should be in the garage! Drove me crazy!

Then there was the remodel I worked on, several years ago, where the owners had to move out because the whole roof had to come off so a second story could be added. The first floor was uninhabitable because the flooring had to be removed so we could add footings for new bearing walls. There was no place for them to hang their hats.

By the way, before the construction starts is a great time to weed through your stuff and have a garage sale or donate to charity. That way there is less stuff to pack, store, or deal with again. Unless you have experience with garage sales, save yourself a lot of time, pick a charity and get rid of your extra stuff. The Disabled American Veterans, Goodwill, Salvation Army or other charitable organization will pick up donations from your home.

The Magic of Tidying Up by Marie Kondo might be a good book for you at this stage of the game. Some of her techniques for getting rid of stuff may be helpful. Also, her ideas on how to arrange things in closets and drawers can save a lot of room in limited storage areas.

Before the construction starts, consider the pets. What are you going to do with them? The strange voices, noises, and smells might upset your pets. Regardless of how diligent the workers are, they may unintentionally let one of your pets out during the construction. On the other side, will the dog's constant barking drive the workers or you crazy?

Protecting Your Property

Speaking of household stuff, before construction starts, or as the first operation of the project, have the contractor protect the house and the personal property. The demolition portion of a construction project is a very dirty, dusty business. You are going to find dust everywhere in your house. Here are a couple of things you should insist that the general contractor do.

1. Have a separate entrance for the workers to keep them out of areas that are not part of the project, if possible.

2. Have a dust barrier put up between project areas and non-project areas. This consists of two pieces of construction plastic sheeting covering openings between the project and non-project areas. If the project areas do not need to be accessed from the non-project areas, a single heavy thickness visqueen, or plastic, firmly taped around the opening, will work well. If an opening is an access point, two sheets of plastic are

overlapped. They are taped at the top and on one side. A 2" by 4" holds down the bottom of the plastic. This provides a simple, efficient airlock. However, dust is still going get into non-project areas.

3. Place your small valuables in a safe, a safe-deposit box, or some other secure location. With the process I have detailed, the general contractor and any subcontractors should be honest individuals. However, one or more of their employees may suffer from a lack of honesty. In most cases, out of sight is out of mind. This is something the property owner must do, not the contractor. This is true for items three through seven.

4. If there is furniture in the home that is very valuable, either monetarily or sentimentally, get it out of the way! Put it in a spare room. Put in a different location. This is something the property owner must do, not the contractor.

5. Protect your furniture. If furniture must be left in a room that is having work done on it, insist that the general contractor cover the furniture with plastic and/or drop cloths.

6. If the workers are going to be pounding on one side of a wall, remove anything hanging on the other side. If there are kitchen cabinets on the other side, empty them. This is something the property owner must do, not the contractor.

7. Videotape or photograph the inside and outside of your house before construction starts. That way if a dispute arises over damage to the house, there is a benchmark for comparison purposes. Also, it is fun to look at the before and

after photographs or videos a few years down
the road. This something the property owner
must do, not the contractor.

Here are a few more things to think about. Does the
property owner have a strict schedule? It is a good idea to give
the general contractor an idea of the family's comings and
goings. Also, let the general contractor know how to get in
touch with you. None of you know when or why that might be
necessary. While we are on the topic of contact, how often do
you want to be contacted by the general contractor? Daily,
weekly, or only when a payment is due or there is a problem?

 Call Before You Dig

A note for those doing-it-yourself: *call before you dig!* In most
areas of the country there are lots pipes for gas, water, electricity,
sewer, and telephone buried under and adjacent to your property. It
can be very expensive to have one of these pipes repaired if you
damage it while digging a hole or trench in your yard. Either call 8-1-1
or go to Call811.com/before-you-dig. Contact them a week or so
before digging.

Do not assume that because nothing is supposed to be buried
under your property that nothing is there. A swimming pool
contractor, on one of my jobs, almost ruptured an 8"-diameter water
pipe. The pipe was supposed to be buried along the property line

between two lots, but it was 7' east of the position shown on the utility maps.

Who Are These People in My House?

The house and property have been protected. Construction has begun. Who are these people who seem to have taken over the home? They are most often men. They will have music blasting from a truck or boom box. They may be a bit more profane than you. Many live "paycheck to paycheck." They wear grubby clothes. They arrive at the crack of dawn and are gone by 4 o'clock. These are the men, and maybe women, who have the expertise to convert your dreams into reality. How should they be treated?

Here are some *don'ts*:

- You don't have to feed them.
- You don't have to give them drinks, but it is reasonable to offer cold water in hot weather.
- Don't ask them about the project. They may not know the project's full scope.
- Don't complain to them.
- Don't give them beer or other alcohol. As a matter of fact, don't let them drink on your property at any time of the day.
- Don't let them do drugs on your property.

- Don't buy anything they may be selling as a side business, and don't sell to them.

Here are some *Do's*:

- Do watch and listen to what is going on.
- Do take notes.
- You may ask them not to smoke on your property.
- You may ask them to turn down the volume of their music, or even turn it *off*.

Local Conditions

Each construction site has its unique conditions. In Southern California, any type of construction can take place any time of the year. In the Northeast, the shell of a building may be erected and closed in by the time the snows start. During the winter, the interior is finished. Any leftover exterior work may be left until the spring.

It is my recommendation that if the outside air temperature at the warmest part of the days is less than 50° F, do not let any concrete be poured after 12:00 noon in areas that do not receive any direct afternoon sunlight. The colder the temperature, the longer it takes concrete to set up. I have worked until midnight finishing concrete on cold days because it wasn't drying.

Many cities have noise abatement laws that limit the permissible noise levels in residential neighborhoods between

10:00 p.m. and 8:00 a.m. This can be a real problem in the desert in the summer, where workers want to start working at the crack of dawn to avoid the hottest part of the day. If the job is in an apartment, condo, or co-op in a high-rise building, the building may have its own noise regulations.

If the job is in an apartment, condo, or co-op in a high-rise building, the construction crews and the material suppliers will need to use the service elevator. the service elevator may have limited hours of operation.

As with noise abatement, some high-rise buildings or condominium developments may have rules that limited the hours during which construction may be performed and/or deliveries received.

Labor unions are stronger in some areas than others. Some buildings and developments may have rules regarding the use of union vs. non-union contractors and subcontractors, though this is more common in commercial buildings than in residential buildings. In some locales, the unions may not be subtle in their displeasure if you use non-union contractors. San Francisco, St. Louis, and New York, among others, are strong union areas.

Construction File

The property owner should keep a construction or project file. Everything related to the remodel goes into the file—everything! Paint chips, bids, the contract, receipts for items purchased by the property owner that the contractor will install—all this paperwork goes into this file.

Can't remember something or something needs to be double-checked? The construction file is the one place to look. My experience says, divide the file and its contents into sections similar to the following:

Design and Architecture
1. Your copy of your contract with the architect
2. Your copies of preliminary drawings
3. Architect's invoices

Samples and Brochures
1. Laminate samples
2. Paint samples
3. Any brochures

Contractor Information and Proposals
1. All correspondence from all the contractors that have had anything to do with your remodel
2. Checklists and notes you have made about any of the contractors
3. All bids (proposals)

The Contract

1. The contract
2. Change orders
3. Invoices and receipts;
4. Preliminary notices
5. Lien releases

Miscellaneous Items—if it doesn't belong anywhere else, put it here

One option would be to put the invoices, receipts, and other payment information into a separate file.

By dividing the file into sections, it is a bit easier to find specific things without having to go through the whole file. It is surprising, the amount of paperwork a project will generate, and how often an item is needed.

Storing Materials and Equipment

Some stages of the construction process require large amounts of materials such as lumber for framing. The materials must be delivered to the jobsite before they can be used. Once the materials arrive, they must be stored somewhere. Most lumber can be stored outside. The contractor may want to cover it with a tarp in damp weather. Drywall should be stored in the area where it will be hung so that it doesn't get wet. Electrical equipment and wire should be kept dry.

Any finish materials and things like appliances and toilets should not be delivered to the job until they can be installed right away. Don't let the contractor purchase things for the end of the job early in the construction unless they have a long lead time. Things get damaged while being stored on the job.

Designate an area of your yard that the contractor can use for staging materials. Until the new area has been secured from the elements, the contractor may ask to use a portion of your garage or carport to store equipment and materials that should be protected from the elements. Don't let the workers take over the yard or your entire garage.

Almost all construction materials can be stored outside. The contractor just needs to lay several pieces of 2" x 4" lumber on the ground, place a piece of plywood over the 2" x 4"s and stack the equipment or materials on the plywood. This will keep ground moisture from getting to the materials. A plastic drop cloth will provide protection from rain or snow.

The Construction Sequence

The job has begun. In what order should things happen? The Construction Sequence List shown in Figure 8 is a list of the general sequence of residential construction. *(This worksheet, as well as other worksheets and checklists, is available in full-size format at no cost, from PeterAKlein.com.)*

This is not an extensive list, but it will cover the sequence for new construction. It is worth noting that parts of the sequence may vary from job to job, and some of the tasks may happen at the same time as other tasks.

For instance, it is very common for the plumber, electrician, and heating contractor to be on the job at the same time. There will need to be coordination between the trades. The plumber, electrician, and heating contractor need to work together so that the electrical outlet and the gas pipe are in the proper places for the furnace the mechanical contractor is installing.

If the kitchen is the sole area being revamped, a lot of these steps will be omitted. For this discussion, let's assume that we are adding a home office to the house. Our sample project will be built slab-on-grade, and the new floor will be level with the existing floor level. The new room will be in line with one existing wall. The existing house has a stucco exterior, which we want to match.

You may wonder what the difference is between rough and finish. In general, the work that is performed during rough-in is never seen after the walls are closed up, but is critical to the operation of the equipment installed during the finish operation.

Construction Sequence List

The list below shows the general sequence of a construction job. This is not hard and fast in a remodel. In a remodel, the same operation may be repeated at different times in different parts of the house. Some of the operations may happen at the same time as others. Some operations may not be included in the project. Inspections are included and shown in bold print.

Prior to the actual construction these items should be completed: Select Architect, Review Preliminary Design Layout, Get Preliminary Bids, Final Design, Get Final Proposals, and Get Building

Clearing: clearing clears any landscaping from the ground where construction is to take place.
Grading: Grading is leveling the ground and raising or lowering the elevation of the building area.
Foundation: Form boards are set in place and leveled. Any underground piping is put in, then the footings are dug, and the pad is leveled if a slab is being poured. Re-bar is installed and tied, and any embeds are positioned.
Foundation Inspection

Pour concrete
Framing: Walls, ceilings, floors, and roofs are built.
Rough Electric: Wiring is run, switch boxes, outlet boxes and lighting boxes are installed in the walls/ceilings/floors.
Rough Plumbing: Piping is run.
Rough Mechanical: ducting is run.
Framing, Rough Electric, Rough Plumbing, and Rough Mechanical Inspections

Roofing: The roofing materials are applied to the roof.
Doors: Doorjambs and doors are installed
Exterior Dry-In: A black, building paper is nailed to the outside of the building to provide a water barrier.
Insulation: Insulation is installed in exterior walls, ceilings, and under floors that are not on slab.
Interior Drywall: Gypsum board sheets are nailed or screwed to the interior walls.
Drywall Nailing Inspection

Drywall Tape and Texture: The heads of nails and the joints are covered with paste and sanded. The finish texture is applied.
Exterior Finish Applied – Siding, Shakes or Stucco (plaster). If stucco is used, it will be applied in three coats: scratch, brown and color. On a small job the scratch and brown might be performed on the same day. If stucco is used, wait 14 days between second and third coats.
Cabinets: Any cabinetry is installed
Painting: Interior walls, unfinished cabinets, exterior fascia, and soffit are painted/stained.

Figure 8-1 Construction Sequence List

Finish Electrical: Lights are installed, outlets, switches, and breakers are installed and activated.
Finish Mechanical: Furnaces, air conditioners, registers, and grills are installed. The systems are tested.
Finish Plumbing: Sinks, faucets, showerheads, etc. are installed.
Flooring: Flooring is installed.
Finish Plumbing: Toilets are installed after the flooring. This way if the toilet has to be replaced the flooring is tight to the toilet flange.
Window Covering: Things like blinds and drapes are installed.
Exterior Patios and Walkways:
Landscaping: Irrigation is installed, and landscaping is planted.
Final Inspection

Figure 8-2 Construction Sequence List (continued)

When plumbing is roughed in, the hot and cold-water pipes are installed in the walls, or wherever they need to run. The waste lines are run from where the sinks, tubs, and other plumbing fixtures will be installed to the sewer line, and the vents are run up to the roof.

During the finish operation, all the plumbing fixtures are installed and hooked up to the supply and waste lines. Flooring should be installed before the toilets are set. If toilets go in first, it may be impossible to find the exact same toilet in the future, and some of the slab or subflooring may be exposed.

Insist that the job be cleaned up at the end of each workday. Keeping a job clean makes it a safer job for all concerned.

Hazardous Materials

A common refrain in the remodeling industry is "You never know what you are going to find until you get the walls open." Until the walls, floors, and ceilings have been opened, the designer and the contractor are basing their work on what they expect to see from years of experience in residential construction.

Once the walls, floors, and ceilings have been opened where the remodel will tie into the existing residence, then the surprises may begin. For instance, at a remodel I did, we needed to open the wall between two rooms. We thought the rooms shared a single wall. Yet, when we opened the wall, we found a gap between the walls. No idea why it was there.

Another surprise can be the discovery of hazardous materials (HazMat.) To illustrate the impact of hazardous materials, let me relate a recent experience of a family member. They bought an older house, moved in, and got settled. Not long after moving in they discovered a leak in the master bathroom. It was not an obvious leak, in that the source was inside a wall, not something easy to see or fix.

Everything that had just been put away in the master bathroom now had to be taken out and put somewhere else. Next, the walls had to be opened to expose the water pipes. Once the walls were opened, three things were found; the leak, asbestos insulation, and black mold. The bad section of pipe was easy to fix, and that was taken care of straightaway. The pipe had been leaking for quite some time, which was the cause of the mold. When the house was built, asbestos insulation was "the" insulation.

The discovery of hazardous materials triggered a HazMat remediation. The first step in remediation is an on-site investigation. Having a floor plan of the remodel and at least that portion of the residence where the remodel with attaches to the existing residence helps the investigating team get an overview of the residence. The investigating team will be dressed in sealed HazMat suits. They will cut holes in walls where they suspect more hazardous materials are located. From each hole they will extract samples of what is behind the walls, bag the samples in sealable bags, and seal the holes.

When the team feels that they have found the limits of the contaminants, they seal off the impacted areas. The samples the investigation team has collected are tested in their laboratory. With the results in hand, a remediation plan is written and implemented.

In the case of asbestos and mold-related problems, the remediation has three basic parts: sealing the hazardous materials to prevent their spread, removing the asbestos, and eliminating the mold. Sealing the impacted area is done with sheets of Visqueen, heavy-grade plastic sheeting, that is taped into place to seal off the contaminated wall sections. Sealing the affected area prevents the damaging spores from getting into the air and being breathed by the home's inhabitants as well as any workers and guests.

The remediation of the asbestos involves collecting all the asbestos, including brushing the insides of the walls for any remnants; placing the asbestos in sealable plastic bags, and then disposing of it all at the proper facility.

Remediation for the mold involves washing the walls with bleach to kill the mold and then drying the areas where the mold used to be. In the case of this family member, the drying took a couple of months with large, noisy floor fans running day and night to aid the drying process.

Once the remediation is complete, the family gets its house back. In this case, the family had homeowner's insurance, which covered the remediation, and the rebuilt bathroom now looks fantastic!

If you are considering remodeling a rental residence that you own, I hope it will not have been a place where the former tenants cooked meth. Meth is a very toxic hazardous material that requires an expensive, exhaustive, and thorough remediation.

Termites

While termites are not considered to be hazardous materials, they can do as much or more damage to a home as any hazardous material. Termite damage may be hidden so that you do not see it. If it has been several years since your house was last inspected or treated for termites, getting a termite inspection before the remodel starts is a good idea. If some termite damage is found, the house can be treated; then any damage can be taken care of as part of the remodel while you have the workers there. (Note: if you do not like the idea of having your home tented, consider orange oil treatment. No tenting and you do not have to move out for a couple days.)

Being Your Own Superintendent

It is suggested that the property owner not function as the job superintendent. Instead, the property owner can write down things that are not understood and ask the general contractor or the superintendent. The more involved the property owner is, the less chance there is of being taken advantage of.

As much as possible, walk through the construction daily and see what is going on. With some trades, it is easy to figure out what should happen. Insulation, for example, is as simple as stuffing the insulation batts between studs, joists, and rafters. Hanging drywall is also easy to understand. The drywall is nailed or screwed to the walls and ceilings.

Framing is much more complicated. Doors and windows need to be located in their proper places. The walls need to be of the correct height. Walls need to be tied together in the proper method for the materials used.

The reader is not expected to learn all about each trade. However, being visible to the workers indicates interest. The property owner can do things like compare the actual door and window locations to the locations indicated on the plans. Check wall heights. Have toilets, sinks, tubs, and other plumbing fixtures been stubbed out in the proper locations? How does one get ready for this? (Stubbed out means that the supply and waste pipes are in their proper places, as are electrical outlets and switch boxes, and they have wire in them.) The Project Inspection Checklist shown in Figure 9 lists things for you to look at as you "inspect" your project. *(This checklist, as well as other worksheets and checklists, is available in full-size format at no cost, from PeterAKlein.com.)*

Project Inspection Checklist

Foundation

All vegetation has been removed from areas where concrete will be poured
Finish grade is smooth and level for a slab.
Rebar is positioned in the footings prior to pouring concrete.
Rebar is epoxied into holes drilled into existing foundation.
Anchor bolts and other hold-downs are positioned in the footings prior to pouring concrete.
Foundation is square, opposite sides are parallel.
For slabs
Heavy gauge plastic (visqueen) is laid over the leveled ground;
Sand is placed over the visqueen;
Metal fabric or rebar mesh is placed on the sand. The metal should form a checkerboard
Slabs are level, no bumps or depressions.

Framing

Lumber is the grade specified in the contract or in the specifications
Doors and windows are in the proper locations and are the proper width and height.
Walls are of the proper height, length and location.
Bearing walls are secured to anchor bolts with washers and nuts.
Studs, joists, and rafters are no more than sixteen inches on center, fourteen and one-half inches
Unless drawn otherwise, walls are at right angles to each other where they meet
There are no bows in the walls.
Trusses, if used, do not touch non-bearing walls.
Joints are tight
Walls are plumb and do not have any bulges.

Ceilings

Rooms that should have flat ceilings have flat ceilings,
Rooms that should have pitched ceilings have pitched ceilings
Skylights are located in the proper locations.
Openings for stairs are in the proper location.

Roof

Skylights are located in the proper locations.
Eaves (overhangs) are the proper width.
Eaves open or closed
Fascia square to rafters or plumb (parallel to walls).
Fascia boards are straight, with tight joints
Roof has proper pitch
Roof material is what is called for in the plans and specifications, and of the proper color.

Figure 9-1 Project Inspection List

Electrical
Lighting is in the proper locations.
Fans are in the proper locations.
Outlets are in the proper locations.
Switches are in the proper locations.
The proper color was used for switches, outlets, and cover plates.

Plumbing
Stub outs for plumbing fixtures are in the proper locations, both hot water, cold water and waste
Metal tape or plates are placed over the top and bottom plates to prevent nails from puncturing the
Copper pipes are not in contact with other metal surfaces.

Mechanical
Ducts are run to the proper rooms.
Thermostat is above a return air grill.
The proper compressor unit and forced air unit (FAU) were installed.

Insulation
All exterior walls are insulated.
All ceilings immediately below the roof are insulated.
All floors on the main level of the dwelling, that are not concrete slab, are insulated.
Insulation fills the entire bay between framing members snugly, but is not bunched up.

Drywall
Nails or screws that missed the framing members have been removed.
Joints are snug and tight.
All nail and/or screw heads are below the surface of the drywall.
All joints are taped.
All nail and/or screw heads are covered with joint compound or taping compound.
Texturing is even.

Stucco / Exterior plaster
Building paper encloses the exterior of the building.
First coat completely covers the lath.
Second coat is smooth throughout.
At least fourteen days have passed between the second coat and the color, third, coat.
Color coat texture should be consistent throughout.
OR
Siding
Building paper encloses the exterior of the building.
Corner and joints are even and smooth.
Trim pieces are installed.

Figure 9-2 Project Inspection List (continued)

Painting
A good quality primer is applied to all raw surfaces that will receive paint.
Doors are sanded between coats.
No gaps, holidays, are left in the final coat.
If you can see the lines of the drywall joints, after the walls have been painted, the walls were not
The proper color or colors were used.

Tile
The proper tile was used.
Tile surfaces are level.
Grout lines are even.
Grouting is sealed.

Cabinetry
The gap between two adjacent doors is even from top to bottom.
No gaps are visible between walls and cabinetry.
Drawer faces are aligned evenly.
Counter tops are level, side-to-side and front-to-back.
There are no mars in any surfaces.

Figure 9-3 Project Inspection List (continued)

Prepare Yourself

Before getting started, go to the library and/or a bookstore and get some books on home construction and home improvement. Become knowledgeable about the process that is about to start. The more you know, the less chance you have of things going wrong. Knowledge is power. You are not expected, in just a few months' time, to become contractors; but you can keep from having the wool pulled over your eyes.

Learn some of the lingo. Construction has a rich vocabulary all its own. In construction, a crown is not something a king wears on his head, nor is it an artificial tooth. It is the natural curvature of a long piece of lumber. Lumber that is installed horizontally, such a ceiling joists, are installed with the crown up so that when flooring and furniture is placed on it, the lumber will level out rather than deflect below level.

As far as the management of the project goes, talk to the general contractor, the general's superintendent, or project manager. This is truer for things pertaining to scheduling, materials, money, and subcontractors. These are things not to discuss with the workers. They won't know.

The general or general's representative should walk your job at least once a day, on days when something is happening. There may be days when nothing will take place. This will happen because one process needs time to dry or cure before something else is added to it. Or it may happen because of scheduling conflicts with other jobs, materials' not arriving on time, or weather delays.

Job schedules can be a touchy subject. Most contractors want to get on and off a job as soon as possible. The longer they are on a job, the less money they make. The general contractor's schedule will be a fair estimate of how long each phase will take and the time duration for the whole project.

One thing to watch for is the roof loading. If a heavy roof is being installed, such as mission tile, roof loading is very important. Let's say a large family room will be added to the house. The existing mission tile roof will be matched. When the roofer starts the roof, a layer of thirty-pound-or-heavier felt is nailed over the plywood roof deck. Felt paper is a heavy-duty felt that is impregnated with asphalt. A 30-pound felt weighs 30 pounds per square. A square is 100 square feet.

After the felt is rolled out and nailed down, the tile is loaded onto the roof on palettes. It is critical that the tile be evenly distributed around the roof. It should not all be stacked in one spot so that weight is concentrated in one area.

Many years ago, I was the architect's inspector at Mission Hills Country Club in Rancho Mirage, California. Soon after the roofing materials had been loaded, I was walking into the garage of one of the condos and noticed that a beam running across the middle of the garage was sagging. I went back outside, got a ladder and went up on the garage roof. The roofing material supplier had loaded the all tile for each roof on the flat garage roof and none on the sloped roof. Mission tile is very heavy!

This caused the beams to sag in each garage. An additional problem could have been that when the tile was distributed over the whole roof, the drywall, which had just been installed, would crack because the condo had not had a chance to settle before the drywall went on.

Loading the roofing materials evenly over the entire roof gives the building a chance to settle. The weight of the roofing materials pushes down on the walls and compresses the framing a little bit. After it has had a few days to settle, the drywall can be hung without worrying about cracking.

Deadlines

Watch out for artificial deadlines. Things like needing or wanting the job done by Christmas, or a wedding. Each step in a construction project takes a certain amount of time. Throwing more people at it may make things worse. If construction cannot be going on a certain date, it is best to start construction after the event. The alternative is to have workers in the house six and seven days a week, if any of them are willing to work overtime. And that does not guarantee construction will be done on time. Keep in mind that not a lot gets done between Christmas and New Year's Day.

The actual construction of the remodel is an exciting time. There are lots of people coming and going. Some trades seem to come and go in the blink of an eye. Others seem like they have moved in with you. At some stages the new area seems huge, and a short time later it seems much too small. Construction is noisy and messy. Construction is when you get to see the realization of all the planning and preparation.

Once again, to help you with the construction sequence, please see Figure 8, Construction Sequence List.

Plans are nothing; Planning is everything.

—Dwight D. Eisenhower

Chapter 9. Construction Documents

Once you have selected someone to prepare the construction documents, what should you expect from the designer? You want enough information so a contractor can prepare a bid for you and execute the construction so you get the remodel you expect. The plans should show the layout of the existing structure as well as the layout of the new or remodeled areas including dimensions. The specifications should spell out the materials to be used, the colors, and the finishes.

How do you know if the designer has given you what you need? In this chapter, designer refers to any person who prepares construction documents.

Construction Documents vs. Contract Documents

At this point it is a good idea to define which documents are construction documents and which are contract documents. Your project may not require all of them.

Construction Documents

The construction documents include the following:

- Plans and specifications, prepared by the designer (drawings and notes of what you want to build)
- Soils report (prepared by a civil engineer)
- Civil engineering documents (public improvements, grading plans, and surveying
- Landscape and irrigation plans and specifications
- Interior design documents (finishes and furnishings)

For a small remodel, the plans (drawings) and specifications may be just a few sheets. The interior design might be covered by the room finish schedule, which will be discussed later in this chapter. All the construction documents are prepared before construction starts. These are the documents that dictate what will happen during construction. These documents are key to the project according to your plans. They must be completed prior to construction so the contractors and suppliers can provide accurate estimates for the project and know what to build. Plus, the construction documents are needed in order to obtain a building permit.

Contract Documents

The contract documents include the construction documents. These four documents comprise the contract documents:

- The written agreement between the owner and contractor
- Addenda
- The construction documents
- Modifications

The written agreement is the contract between the property owner and the general contractor for construction services. The written agreement should include and incorporate all the other three documents. The written agreement between the owner and contractor itemizes the scope of the project and the responsibilities of both parties. It is a contract, so it must be reviewed with care before signing.

Addenda detail the changes made to the construction documents prior to signing the written agreement—things that come to light during the bidding process. Addenda encompass any changes to any of the other documents, prior to the contract signing. Often these include changes due to corrections from the building department before a permit is issued.

The construction documents have already been discussed. Modifications are revisions made after the written agreement has been signed. These come in the form of change orders. They can be instigated by either party and may be mandatory or optional.

For example, a mandatory change may be having to jackhammer up a sidewalk to replace a master water valve that could not be opened after being shut off to work on water pipes in an existing building.

An example of an optional item could be when the owner walked into the house while the framing was underway and wanted a window added in a certain spot.

As the scope of the project changes, there will be a proportional change in the number and complexity of the documents.

What Is Enough?

Had a remodel that was built from a set of plans totaling two 24" x 36" sheets. Those plans, while meeting the requirements of the City of San Diego, didn't answer all the questions. On top of that, the husband and wife couldn't agree on many of the items that had to be selected during the course of construction—items that should have been selected before the contract was signed. This caused delays while we waited for decisions from the owners. The accumulated delays caused the project completion to be pushed back by a whole month. Is this what you want?

What you should get is a set of plans that includes a layout of the area to be remodeled and also tells a contractor where the property is located; where the project is in relation to the existing structure and the property lines; how the foundation and walls should be built; where the electrical, plumbing and mechanical will be altered; and how the finished remodel will look and be built.

A small, straightforward room addition requires a smaller set of plans than a larger, two-story addition on a hill that needs a special foundation. One building department may have less stringent requirements than another building department.

Most building departments have minimum sizes for the various drawings, or plans, that are required for obtaining a building permit. Most designers draw plans on 24" x 36" sheets of paper, so this should not be a problem. If you decide to draw your own plans, check with your local building department for the plan sizes they require.

The Minimum Set

Let's use The City of La Mesa, California, as an example. La Mesa requires a site or plot plan, a floor plan, exterior elevations, a building section, a foundation plan, a roof framing plan, floor framing plan if the new floor is not on a slab, an electrical plan, a mechanical plan, a plumbing plan, and general notes. Electrical, mechanical, and plumbing plans are required if any electrical, mechanical, or plumbing is being added or modified. Other jurisdictions may have different requirements.

Note that building departments are not concerned about colors, finishes, and textures, whereas planning departments might be.

For most jurisdictions, the following sections discuss the most common requirements.

Plot Plan

A site or plot plan is a plan or overhead view showing your lot boundaries, how the existing house sits on the lot, and where the remodel or addition will be. It should include the street address, the assessor's parcel number, and a legal description of the lot. The remodeled area should be shown in different background pattern or shading than the existing structure.

Distinguishing the new structure from the old structure is helpful to the building officials as well anyone who must bid on your project or work on it.

Floor Plan

The floor plan is an overhead view of the layout of the building, including dimensions. Most floor plans are drawn at a scale of one quarter inch (¼") to the foot. The drafter will differentiate existing areas from new areas. The floor plan influences all the other drawings.

Foundation Plan

The foundation plan will show the areas that get new foundations. It is also drawn at a scale of one quarter inch to the foot. The sheet that has the foundation plan may also have one or more foundation details. These details show the concrete contractor how deep to dig the footings, how wide the footings should be, and what types of reinforcement, embedded items, and other details are needed to ensure that the proper foundation is built.

Other Plans

The architect uses the finalized floor plan to draw a foundation plan; roof and floor framing plans; electrical, mechanical, and plumbing plans; and elevations. The floor plan will tell the architect where new footings are needed, how the electrical system should be laid out, and how the exterior will look. A roof framing plan shows how the roof should be built. This is useful where there are several ridges and valleys.

Exterior Elevations

Exterior elevations show how the house will look from the outside. An elevation is a view from the side, whereas a plan looks down on the house or building from above. If you were adding a room to the back of your home, you should have one to three exterior elevations. If the new room adjoins the existing dwelling on the south, you would have exterior elevations of the south, east, and west sides.

Building Sections

A section shows what the building should look like if it were cut vertically and you were shown a cutaway drawing from one end to the other. In some cases, a portion of the cutaway may be all that is shown. A section shows such things as wall framing, floor, ceiling and roof framing, foundation, and insulation. Sections are often drawn at one-quarter-inch-to-the-foot scale or larger.

Details

There will probably be some additional details showing how different parts of the structural system tie together. A typical detail would show how a typical wall is secured to the foundation with anchor bolts, washers, and nuts. Details are drawn at a larger scale than might be used a plan or elevation.

Electrical, Mechanical, and Plumbing Plans

An electrical plan shows the location of ceiling- and wall-mounted lights, light switches, electrical outlets, cable and telephone outlets, and the main service panel and any sub-panels. It is now common for houses to have wiring installed for computer networks. This would also be shown on the electrical plan.

A mechanical plan shows the layout of the heating, ventilation, and air conditioning systems. The mechanical plan will show the location of the furnace, air conditioners, supply ducts, and return-air ducts.

A plumbing plan shows the location of plumbing fixtures and the flow of the various waste and supply pipes.

On small jobs it is common for the electrical, mechanical, and plumbing plans to be drawn on the same page; or they may be included on the floor plan in many instances.

Some sets of plans may also include interior elevations. Interior elevations are used to show how cabinets will be laid out.

General Notes

Most architects will fill up a page with general notes, such as how shear panels and the roof sheathing should be nailed to the studs or rafters.

The plans mentioned so far constitute the minimum set for submission to the building department. The minimum set of construction documents from which a bid could be developed would include specifying all the finish materials to be used on the project.

The minimum set of plans from which you could obtain a building permit would be a set of plans that is compliant with the local building codes. If any corrections were needed, they would have been made prior to permit issuance.

A complete set of construction documents from which you could build would include everything being specified, including allowances for things like carpets and draperies. All the specifications concerning materials and finishes should be with the owner's (your) approval.

If you wanted to have the rest of your house painted as part of the remodel, that would be added to the notes and specifications. The construction documents should reflect everything that is to be done to the house as part of the project.

Schedules

Schedules are an important part of the construction documents, as they list details for specific areas or treatments. The three most common schedules are the door schedule, the window schedule, and the room finish schedule.

The door schedule lists each door that is new or is being replaced. The door number corresponds to the door number on the floor plan. The schedule lists each door's width, height, and thickness; its core (hollow or solid); if it is pre-hung; whether it is paint or stain grade; and, if there is any glass in the door, the number of pieces, size, and shape. If you are ordering a specific door from a catalog or building material supplier, the manufacturer and the model number should be included.

The window schedule lists similar items for each new or replaced window. In the window schedule you see a letter instead of a number. The letter corresponds to the window letter on the plans. For each window you will see the size (width, then height), whether it is fixed or not, the frame material and color, the color of the glass, and if it is dual glazed.

The room finish schedule, which may include the flooring schedule, will tell what material finishes are to be applied to the floor, walls, and ceiling in each room that is part of the project. The living room may call for walls with orange-peel texture and flat paint, and the ceiling is to have a sprayed acoustic texture. A bathroom may call for smooth textured walls and ceiling and eggshell enamel paint.

Notes

Notes are details that are important, such as key players in the project and their contact information. This might include the landscape architect, the structural engineer, and the interior designer.

Clarity

Whoever draws your plans should deliver to you a set of construction documents that includes plans, schedules, and notes that are clean, legible, and clear. *Clean* means that the lines are sharp and precise. *Legible* means that the lettering is easily readable. *Clear* means that there is not a lot of background color on areas that do not have notes or drawings on them.

The better and more inclusive the construction documents, the easier it is for the contractors to accurately bid your job. It will make building the remodel easier for all concerned. You should get construction documents that, at a bare minimum, meet the requirements of the building department for your jurisdiction.

Specifications

The specifications, or *specs* as they are often called, are a separate document that clarifies various parts of the plans and are divided into 16 sections. For example, suppose the plans show a new slab is to be poured for the new room. The architect, in Division 3 of the specifications, would write, in detail, the requirements of the concrete to be used for the project. In Division 9, the acceptable brands of paint would be listed. On a smaller remodel, the specifications may be included in the plans.

Division 01 — General Requirement

Division 02 — Site Construction

Division 03 — Concrete

Division 04 — Masonry

Division 05 — Metals

Division 06 — Wood and Plastics

Division 07 — Thermal and Moisture Protection

Division 08 — Doors and Windows

Division 09 — Finishes

Division 10 — Specialties

Division 11 — Equipment

Division 12 — Furnishings

Division 13 — Special Construction

Division 14 — Conveying Systems

Division 15 — Mechanical / Plumbing

Division 16 — Electrical

As-Builts

You will want one additional set of plans, but they will not be available until the construction is complete. These are called *As-Builts*. As the name indicates, As-Builts show how the job was built, reflecting any deviations from the approved plans.

The contractor should use a red pencil and draw the variances on the approved plans. Perhaps an access panel needed to be moved because of the layout of the ceiling joists or a pipe. The As-Builts should stay with the house when you sell. That will give the new owner an idea of how things were built. In some jurisdictions, the building department may want a set of the As-Builts.

The construction documents should spell out the entire story of your remodel. Think of it as a script. All the workers will take their cues from the construction documents. Make your decisions before the designer has completed the design and the construction documents.

It takes hands to build a house, but only hearts can build a home.

—Pinterest

Chapter 10. Permits and Inspections

Not every home improvement project requires a building permit. Suppose the kitchen cabinets are to be refaced and the house is to be repainted. This work does not require a permit. This is because nothing is being done that impacts the structure of the house nor the electrical, mechanical, and plumbing systems.

The policies of the City of La Mesa, California, will serve as an example. The following projects do not need a permit:

- One-story detached accessory buildings used as tool and storage sheds in residential zones, playhouses, tree houses, and similar uses, provided the floor area does not exceed 100 square feet.
- Playground, gymnastic, and similar equipment and structures used for recreation and athletic activities.
- Fences not over 6' high, which do not enclose a swimming pool.
- Oil derricks.

- Movable cases, counters, and partitions not over 5' 9" high.

- Retaining walls not exceeding 4' in height, measured from the bottom of the footing to the top of the wall, unless supporting a surcharge or impounding Class I, II, or III-A liquids.

- Water tanks supported directly upon grade if the capacity does not exceed 5000 gallons and the ratio of height to diameter or width does not exceed two to one.

- Replastering/re-siding of an existing building.

- Reroofing an existing building if the new roofing material is not heavier than the existing roofing material.

- Installing dual-glazed ICC-approved skylights up to 48" x 48".

- Irrigation systems when installed with a backflow preventer.

- Fences and freestanding masonry walls not over 6' in height.

When Is a Building Permit Required?

For just about everything else, a permit is needed. If the project will affect the structure of the house or the electrical, mechanical, and plumbing systems, or a pool is to be built, a permit is absolutely required. For most projects, several permits may be required, or what the City of San Diego calls a *combination permit.*

If a room is to be added to the home, a basic permit will be needed, which covers the structure. An electrical permit is required for the electrical work. If plumbing is involved, a plumbing permit will be required. A mechanical permit is needed for heating, ventilation and air conditioning (HVAC.) Pools require their own permits, as well as plumbing and electrical permits.

Other building departments have similar policies. Check with the building department that has jurisdiction over the neighborhood where your project is located to get their policies.

Why do cities require building permits in the first place? Permits are required to protect you. A building permit sets a process in motion to ensure that each project follows the applicable building codes.

Think building codes are not important or make construction costs too expensive? Consider this story from the *San Diego Union-Tribune* of December 17, 2007:

> *Long Beach*—A seven-year old girl burned in an apartment fire that killed her two sisters died Saturday after being hospitalized in critical condition.
>
> "Jocelin Aviles suffered several heart attacks after the Friday morning blaze in a converted garage apartment that left her burned over 18 percent of her body," fire officials said.
>
> Jocelin's sisters Stephanie, 6, and Jasmin, 10, died Friday at St. Mary's Medical Center.
>
> "Investigators suspected the fire was started by a portable heater plugged into an overloaded power

strip," said Long Beach Fire Department spokesman Mike DuRee.

The garage had been illegally converted into an apartment and did not have a smoke detector or sprinkler.

Building Codes

What is a building code? Building codes are standards to which all buildings of a given type must conform. In the United States, the International Code Council (ICCsafe.org) drafts and publishes the code used throughout the United States and many other countries. The code is broken down into several volumes, including Building, Fire, Plumbing, and Electrical. Codes are always in a state of flux and updates. Every three years, a new edition is published, with the various volumes being updated on a staggered schedule.

In California, the state adopts the latest ICC codes and requires that *all* local building departments adopt the state codes on January 1 of a specified year. The latest versions are the 2017 codes, which went into effect on January 1, 2018.

What causes a code to be updated? Disasters! Every time we have a major earthquake in California, structural engineers study the structures that failed in order to figure what was deficient in those structures' design. Once they have pinpointed a cause, they then figure out how to prevent this type of failure from occurring in the future. Once they have that information, they revise the appropriate sections of the building code. Those changes get published with the next update.

We have seen changes to the building and fire codes in the aftermath of the terrorist attacks on the World Trade Towers. Wind-load capacities have been increased since Hurricane Katrina.

Let me give some examples of the things included in codes that keep us safe.

Many of us have a furnace in a closet. The closet does not have an exterior wall. If the furnace is gas fired, the gas must be piped to the furnace. The plumbing code requires that the gas pipe be run above the ceiling rather than under the floor. This keeps houses from being blown off their foundations in the event of a gas leak that causes an explosion.

Another requirement is that specially treated lumber must be used in situations where lumber comes in contact with concrete or masonry. This prevents the lumber from corroding, which could cause the house to fall off the slab or foundation.

A third requirement in residential construction is that electrical outlets be placed every twelve feet in a room. This lessens the need for extension cords. Extension cords have two problems: We trip over them, and they are prone to overheating and causing fires if too many things are plugged into them.

Building codes are written to protect us. It is the architect's job to draw the plans to conform to the latest codes. It is the building department's job to ensure that the plans are drawn to code, and that the contractor follows the plans and codes.

Jurisdictions

Cities and counties have building departments. The city building departments handle permits and inspections for that city. There is no crossover, other than when a larger city's inspectors cover for a small city when its sole inspector is on vacation. Some small cities may contract their building services from a larger neighbor. All unincorporated areas of a county are covered by the county's building department.

The Permitting Process

Once a project's plans have been completed, the homeowner, the architect, or a permit service must take copies of the plans to the appropriate building department. An application for a building permit is filled out. Many jurisdictions charge a plan-check fee in addition to a permit fee. The plans are left at the building department for review, also known as *plan check*.

Depending on the size of the city and the number of projects ahead of yours, the review may take weeks. The plan checkers review the plans to ensure that they are complete and that they comply with the zoning laws and building codes in force in your locale.

The plan checkers will find some corrections. The architect makes the required changes, and the plans are resubmitted. The plan checkers make sure the corrections are complete and then approve the plans. Be forewarned that the permit process can be long and expensive.

Fees

Now the building department is ready to issue the building permit. A check is made out to the appropriate agency, the city or the county. In California, the fees are broken down into two categories: permit fees and school fees. The permit fees are calculated using different methods in different jurisdictions.

Again, we'll use the City of La Mesa as an example. La Mesa determines the permit fees by calculating the square footage of the improvement and then multiplying the square footage by a multiplier. The multiplier for dwellings is $66.00.

Next, the product of the square footage times the multiplier is looked up on a chart. The product is called the valuation. Let's say that the valuation is $10,000.00. The plan check fee is $99.58, and the building permit fee is $153.20, for a total of $252.78.

CAL In California, Proposition 13 ("Prop 13") limits property taxes on residential property to 1% of the assessed value of the property. It also limits the reassessment of residential property when the property changed hands or when it is remodeled.

Before Prop 13, school districts derived much of their income from property taxes. Prop. 13 has had a major negative impact on the physical plant of schools in California. To remedy the situation, the state legislature passed a law that allows school districts to impose fees as part of building permits. This somewhat makes up the lost revenue. California state law spells out how much the districts can charge. These fees are called school fees.

Since school district boundaries and city boundaries often overlap, one building department may collect school fees for more than one school district. For example, the City of La Mesa and the City of Lemon Grove collect school fees for both the La Mesa–Spring Valley School District and the Grossmont Union High School District. The City of El Cajon collects school fees for three school districts. The City of San Diego has a unified district, so a single fee is collected. The school fees are imposed for any additions covering more than 499 square feet. In La Mesa, the La Mesa Spring Valley School District charges $1.27 per square foot. The Grossmont Union

High School District charges $1.03 per square foot. If you add 500 or more square feet, you do not get the first 500 feet free.

Once the fees have been paid, the plans are stamped with the same number as the permit. A copy of the permit, an inspection card, and one copy of the approved or stamped plans is given to whoever obtains the permit.

As a homeowner, do not obtain (pull) your own permit. Let the designer, the general contractor, or a permit service pull the permit. They know the routine; they may know some or all the people handling the plan check and how to work with them. There have been too many instances of homeowners trying to pull their own permits and getting frustrated, which leads to complaining and yelling. Neither does any good and may, in fact, hinder the permit process.

CAL   Permit Triggers Reassessment

One thing property owners in California should know is that once a building permit has been obtained for a remodel, the building department will forward the information to the County Tax Assessor's office. The property taxes will go up. The whole property will not be reassessed, just the remodeled area or improvement. This may be the case in other states as well.

The Inspection Card and Approved Plans

The inspection card and the approved plans received from the building department must stay on the job until the final inspection has been passed. The building inspector will need the inspection card at each inspection, if the inspection is passed. The inspector may need to review the approved plans during the inspection. Plus, these plans are what the building department expects to see constructed.

Every effort should be made to protect the approved plans and inspection card from the construction and from the elements. The inspection card should be stored in a plastic sheet protector. A contractor I know places the approved plans and the inspection card in a 3'-long piece of 3"-diameter ABS pipe capped at both ends, with one end having a screw on cap. This protects the plans from the elements and keeps plans and the inspection card together.

Common Inspections

Inspections are how building departments ensure that the builder is adhering to the building codes. At certain stages of the construction, the builder calls the building department and requests one or more inspections. In most cases, the building department sends a building inspector to the job within 24 hours. Some building departments let the contractor request a morning or afternoon inspection. Others will just confirm what day they will be make the inspection and between what times the inspectors are in the field. During an inspection, an onsite review of the construction is conducted.

Building inspectors are educated in the building codes and construction practices. Their training comes from a combination of construction experience and coursework in building codes. Building inspectors seem to come in two flavors: nitpickers and all the rest. Some will always find something wrong. The rest of the inspectors will pass a job if they don't see any glaring errors.

If possible, it is a good idea for you, the property owner, to walk the job with the building inspector at each inspection. The property owner will learn a bit more about the construction of the remodel, and it shows the inspector concern and involvement.

Following is a list of the most common building inspections, what the inspection covers, and when it is requested:

Foundation—inspects forms, footings, and embeds; requested before concrete is poured.

Note: the next five inspections (framing, rough electrical, rough plumbing, rough mechanical, and roof nailing) may be performed at the same time.

Framing—inspects the frame of the remodeled areas; requested after the framing is completed.

Rough electrical—inspects the wiring and electric panels and checks for minimum number of outlets in each room; requested after framing is completed and rough wiring has been installed.

Rough plumbing—inspects piping and ensures that the lines hold pressure; requested after the framing is completed and the rough ducting has been installed.

Rough mechanical—inspects heating, ventilation, and air conditioning ducts and duct insulation; requested after framing is completed and rough ducting has been installed.

Roof nailing—inspects the nailing pattern of the roof deck; requested after the roof deck has been nailed to the rafters or joists.

Insulation—inspects that the insulation is the proper size for the wall, ceiling, and/or floor; the building department may accept a certificate from the insulation contractor. Inspection requested as soon as insulation has been installed.

Lath—inspects the nailing of the metal lath onto which plaster is applied; requested when lath is completed.

Drywall nailing—inspects the nailing pattern of the drywall; requested after the drywall has been installed but before taping begins.

Final—inspects everything; requested when job is nearly complete.

Ask questions of the inspector, but don't interfere with the inspection. If the inspector fills out a correction notice, ask the inspector to explain the problem. Don't be nasty, just conversational. The explanation will add to your construction knowledge as an owner and will help make sure the contractor makes the proper correction(s).

If the inspector is satisfied with the job, the inspection card will be signed and dated for each inspection performed that day. If you, the property owner, were able to chat with the inspector or saw that the inspection card was signed or a correction notice was left, you should call the general contractor after the inspector leaves.

The call will save the contractor some time. The contractor will know, from the information provided about the inspection, what the next steps will be. If the job passed, the next phase can be started; otherwise, the proper personnel need to return to the job to correct the deficiencies.

Failing a building inspection is not the end of the world. The inspector will fill out a correction notice and leave it on the job with the inspection card. When you call the contractor with the bad news, read the correction notice to them. Then the general can get the proper workers back to the job to make the corrections. Then the building department is called for a reinspection.

Bringing Residences Up to Code

Sometimes parts of an older house must be brought up to current code, where the remodel impacts the dwelling. For instance, this may require that additional smoke detectors be installed in each bedroom. Before my latest remodel, there was one smoke detector in the house. Now there are eight.

A note on smoke detectors: an ionization smoke alarm is generally more responsive to flaming fires, whereas a photoelectric smoke alarm is generally more responsive to smoldering fires.

If bedroom windows will be replaced as part of a remodel, the sills of the replacement windows should be no higher than 42" above the floor. This allows the window to be used as an emergency exit in case of a fire. This is an instance of the building code's being changed as the result of many fire investigations.

Another thing we were required to do was put house numbers in a prominent location in the front of the house. This makes it easier for emergency response personnel to find an address. This was required even though we had the house number painted on the curb.

The permitting process is designed to ensure the safety of the occupants of buildings. Building departments enforce the building codes. Building departments require that plans for building be reviewed before construction begins. Once a set of plans has been approved, a building permit is issued. During the construction of a building, the building department inspects the construction to insure adherence to the building codes.

Your words are building blocks of which you
construct your life and future.

—Charles Capps

Chapter 11. The Contract

You have weeded through all the contractors and selected one.
Now it's time to put a contract together. This is most often done
by the general contractor. The contract is the third piece of the
construction documents. A well-written contract is one of the
best weapons to protect yourself. The contract is a textual
picture of your project.

Get It in Writing

If the contract, or any other component of the construction
documents, is not in writing, it is worthless! *Get the contract in
writing—no ifs, ands, or buts.* In the event you wind up in
arbitration or in court, the written contract is more valuable than
your idea of what was in an oral contract.

Many contracts used by contractors are a single page
with very little space for the description of the work to be

performed and the exclusions. The contractor will write in the barest essentials and give you a copy of the contract to sign.

At the other end of the contract spectrum is the American Institute of Architects (AIA) contract. The AIA contract: Standard Form of Agreement Between Owner and Contractor contains just about everything described in this chapter. It is eight pages long and includes several references to other documents that are considered part of the contract, such as the plans and specifications. While the AIA contract may seem rather long, the AIA has years of experience dealing with contractors. They have learned from this experience and codified that experience.

In the middle is something that the contractor types up on their computer. Have your attorney review it. If your attorney approves the contractor's contract, use it, assuming it contains the items suggested in this chapter. The more explicit the contract, the better for everyone involved, including the contractor. Further proof you have an honest contractor.

CAL   California law requires a much longer contract than most other states. A great deal of this additional verbiage has to do with the rights of laborers, subcontractors, and material suppliers under the mechanic's lien laws of California; the property owner's obligations; and options. This is meant to emphasize the importance of making sure that the subcontractors and suppliers get paid.

The Contract Form

Your agreement with the contractor you selected should be in writing. "Fine," you say, "but what should be in the contract?" Figure 10 provides a sample contract, including a sample Exhibit A. This contract assumes that the owner is going to add a family room to the house—a basic room with some windows, a sliding glass door, and an interior door to separate the room from the rest of the house. This sample shows the detail needed to cover even a simple project. In this section is a list of the items that I feel should be included in your contract with your general contractor.

Identifying information.

a. Date of contract

b. The contractor's business name. This could be the contractor's name, a Fictitious Business Name (FBN, also known as a DBA, for "Doing Business As") or the name of a corporation.

c. The name of the person or persons financially responsible for the remodel. This is most often the owner or owners.

Article 1. Scope of the Work

a. Full address of the property where the work will take place. Adding the legal description shouldn't hurt. The legal description will be something like Lot 3 Block 54 Tract 77 or Parcel 6 Map 35673. The legal description should be in the deed for the property.

b. A detailed description of the scope of the work to be performed. This could be on a separate page or pages (addendum), entitled Exhibit A in the example. This would be a very detailed description to the extent that anything that hasn't been covered in the plans and specifications should be described here. The less detail in the plans and specifications, the more detail should be included in the Scope of the Work.

Also, in the Scope of the Work paragraph or paragraphs, reference the plans and specifications, who designed them, the date of the final drawings and specifications, and the designer's project number or drawing number or the name of the homeowner.

Article 2. Time of Completion

a. The approximate start date of the work.

b. The approximate end date of the work.

c. A description of what constitutes substantial commencement. It is not just having some materials delivered to the job site. You want measurable benchmarks so you and the contractor can both agree that the job has started.

d. A description of what constitutes substantial completion. Passing the final inspection does not mean the job is done. You want measurable benchmarks so you and the contractor can both agree when the job is complete, such as property owner's acceptance of completion of the final punch list.

Article 3. The Contract Price—the price for the labor and materials to complete the job, typed in as words and as a number.

Article 4. Progress Payments—a payment schedule.

a. 10% of the contract price is the maximum down payment you want to make. It doesn't matter what the contractor calls it. Whether a down or a deposit, the maximum you should pay is 10%. If you live outside of California, see if there are similar limits in your state. Check with an attorney, not a contractor, in those states.

CAL   The California State Contractors License Board limits the contractor to a down payment of $1,000 or 10% of the total price of the project, whichever is less. Considering today's costs, this is outdated.

b. Remember: Money talks! The reason you spell out, in detail, what constitutes substantial completion is so you know when to make the final payment.

c. *Never* pay cash for anything!

d. For each check you write, get a receipt from the contractor.

Article 5. General Provisions

a. Who provides the plans (drawings) and specifications.

b. Who obtains the building permits: the designer, the contractor, or the homeowner?

c. A detailed explanation of the contractor's warranty and guarantee for the job, including the warranty duration.

Article 6. Other Terms

a. This is the section where clauses may be added to the agreement that may be required by your state, suggested by your lawyer, agreed upon by you and the contractor, or suggested by the designer.

b. If you don't have room to write or type in all the Other Terms you need, those items may need to be put into an addendum that is referenced in the Other Terms paragraph.

The three items listed in this sidebar are suggestions that you may want to add to the Other Terms of your agreement:

- A stipulation that if arbitration can't resolve your differences, the prevailing party absorbs the other's legal fees.

- A clause stating that the place of litigation shall be in the homeowner's state and the homeowner's county or parish.

- An integration clause to prohibit adding or changing the contract except in limited ways.

Stipulate if any bonds are required, what type of bond or bonds, and to what dollar limit. (Bonds are discussed later in this chapter.)

7. Signatures

a. Witnesses present at the Contract Agreement signing will affix their signatures here.

CAL The name and registration number of any salesperson that solicited or negotiated the contract. (California law restricts the amount paid to a salesperson to a prorated basis of the progress payments as they are made.)

b. The street address, city, state, zip code, and telephone number of the contractor will appear here. If your locale requires that contractors be licensed or registered, then the contractor's license or registration number should be noted on the contract.

c. Appearing here will be signatures of the contractor and the homeowner and date signed.

CAL The 50 states vary greatly in their implementation of mechanic's lien laws. The discussion of mechanic's lien laws in this book is based on California law. Check with your attorney before signing the Contractor Agreement.

d. In my opinion, lien releases should be required and provided to you from all the suppliers, subcontractors, and the general contractor's laborers for work provided up to the point in time of the invoice. (See Chapter 12.) Lien releases should accompany each payment request or invoice.

e. Any penalty clauses. These might include a deduction in the final payment if the project goes beyond a certain date, excluding strikes, weather, or material delays. If you include penalties, you will need to add an incentive clause as well. An incentive might be a bonus to the contractor if the job is finished a certain number of days early.

f. Exclusions. These are things that the contractor has not included in their bid to you. Perhaps the permit fees are excluded. Or maybe landscaping is not a part of the contract. Exclusions are almost as important as inclusions. They help define the scope of the project and help eliminate differences of opinion at a later date.

g. A clause that requires the job to be cleaned up at the end of each workday.

h. If the contractor has promised that the workers on your project will be limited to their in-house employees and you want that to be enforced, add a clause stating that the general contractor cannot use any unlicensed subcontractors.

At PeterAKlein.com you may obtain, at no cost, a copy of the Contract Items (shown here as Figure 11). It lists the items I feel should be in your contract with the general contractor. Other free worksheets and checklists are also available on the website.

(Sample Contract)

CONTRACTOR AGREEMENT

THIS AGREEMENT made the 10th day of February, 2018 by and between Honest John Contracting, hereinafter called the Contractor and Fred and Wilma Flintstone hereinafter called the Owner.

WITNESSETH, that the Contractor and the Owner for the considerations named agree as follows:

ARTICLE 1.   SCOPE OF THE WORK
The Contractor shall furnish all materials and perform all the work shown on the drawings drawn by Artie Architect, and labeled project 2001-01-Flintstone and described in the specifications entitle Exhibit A, as annexed hereto as it pertains to work to be performed on property at:
        1234 Bedrock Boulevard, Bedrock
        Legal Description: Parcel 5, Map 00000 recorded 01-01-1900

ARTICLE 2.   TIME OF COMPLETION
The work to be performed under this Contract shall be commenced on or before March 1, 2018, and shall be substantially completed on or before June 1, 2018.
Time is if the essence. The following constitutes substantial completion of work pursuant to this proposal and contract:
All items set forth in Exhibit A have been completed, Final Inspection has been received, Certificate of Occupancy received from building department, Unconditional Waiver and Release of Liens from all subcontractors, laborers, and material suppliers, Inspection Card, Approved Plans, "As-Built" drawings and user manuals from all contractor installed equipment received by owner.

ARTICLE 3.   THE CONTRACT PRICE
The Owner shall pay the Contractor for material and labor to be performed under the Contract the Sum of Forty - Five Thousand Two Hundred Eighty - Three And No/100 Dollars ($45,283.00), subject to additions and deductions pursuant to authorized change orders.

ARTICLE 4.   PROGRESS PAYMENTS
Payments of the Contract Price shall be paid in the manner following:

Down payment of	$ 1,000.00.
Foundation payment of	$10,000.00.
Framing payment of	$ 7,500.00.
Rough Electric payment of	$ 2,500.00.
Roof payment of	$ 2,500.00.
Doors and Windows payment of	$ 1,500.00.
Insulation payment of	$ 1,500.00.
Drywall payment of	$ 2,783.00.
Stucco scratch coat payment of	$ 1,000.00.
Stucco brown coat payment of	$ 1,000.00.
Stucco color coat payment of	$ 2,000.00.
Painting payment of	$ 2,000.00.
Flooring payment of	$ 5,471.70.
Final payment of	$ 4,528.30.

ARTICLE 5.   GENERAL PROVISIONS

Figure 10-1 Sample Contract (page 1)

All work shall be completed in a workman-like manner and in compliance with all building codes and other applicable laws.

The ~~Contractor~~ / Owner (choose one) shall furnish a plan and scale drawing showing the shape, size dimensions, and construction and equipment specifications for home improvements, a description of the work to be done and description of the materials to be used and the equipment to be used or installed and the agreed consideration for the work.

To the extent required by law all work shall be performed by individuals duly licensed and authorized by law to perform said work.

Contractor may at its discretion engage subcontractors to perform work hereunder, provided Contractor shall fully pay said subcontractor and in all instances remain responsible for the proper completion of this Contract.

Contractor shall furnish Owner appropriate releases or waivers of lien for all work performed or materials provided at the time the next periodic payment shall be due.

All change orders shall be in writing and signed both by Owner and Contractor, and shall be incorporated in, and become a part of the contract.

Contractor warrants it is adequately insured for injury to its employees and others incurring loss or injury as a result of the acts of Contractor or its employees or subcontractors.

~~Contractor / Owner~~ / Designer (choose one) shall at its own expense obtain all permits necessary for the work to be performed.

Contractor agrees to remove all debris and leave the premises in broom clean condition.

In the event Owner shall fail to pay any periodic or installment payment due hereunder, Contractor may cease work without breach pending payment or resolution of any dispute.

All disputes hereunder shall be resolved by binding arbitration in accordance with rules of the American Arbitration Association.

Contractor shall not be liable for any delay due to circumstances beyond its control including strikes, casualty or general unavailability of materials.

Contractor warrants all work for a period of Twelve (12) months following completion.

FAILURE BY CONTRACTOR WITHOUT LAWFUL EXCUSE TO SUBSTANTIALLY COMMENCE WORK WITHIN TWENTY (20) DAYS FROM THE APPROXIMATE START DATE SPECIFIED IN THE PROPOSAL AND CONTRACT WHEN WORK WILL BEGIN IS A VIOLATION OF THE CONTRACTOR'S LICENSE LAW.

ARTICLE 6.   OTHER TERMS

The following terms and conditions apply to the payment schedule in Article 4:

If the payment schedule contained in the contract provides for a down payment to be paid to Contractor by Owner before the commencement of work, such down payment shall not exceed One Thousand Dollars ($1000) or 10 % of the contract price, excluding finance charges, whichever is the lesser.

In no event shall the payment schedule provide for Contractor to receive, nor shall Contractor actually receive, payment in excess of 100% of the value of the work performed on the project at any time, excluding finance charges, except that the Contractor may receive an initial down payment authorized by condition (a) above.

A failure by Contractor without lawful excuse to substantially commence work within twenty (20) days of the approximate date specified in this Contract when work will begin shall postpone the next succeeding payment to Contractor for that period of time equivalent to the time between when substantially commencement was to have occurred and when it did occur.

The terms and conditions set forth in sub-paragraphs (a), (b), and (c) above pertaining to the payment schedule shall not apply when the contract provides for Contractor to furnish a performance and payment bond, lien and completion bond, bond equivalent, or joint control approved by the Registrar of Contractors covering full performance and completion of the contract and such bonds or joint control is or are furnished by Contractor, or when the parties agree for full payment to be made upon or for a schedule of payments to commence after satisfactory completion of the project.

Figure 10-2 Sample Contract (page 2)

when the parties agree for full payment to be made upon or for a schedule of payments to commence after satisfactory completion of the project.

If the contract provides for a payment of a salesperson's commission out of the contract price, that payment shall be made on a pro rata basis in proportion to the schedule of payments made to the contractor by the disbursing party.

WARNING

Do not use this form if the Owner is going to pay interest or nay finance charge. A Home Improvement Contract with finance charges must comply both with the California Retail Installment Sales (Unruh) Act and the Federal Truth in Lending Act. The Federal Truth in Lending Act also applies if the contract price is payable in more than four installments, even if there are no interest or finance charges. (Note: Progress payments are not installment payments.)

Do not use this form is this is a contractor for a swimming pool.

NOTICE TO OWNER
(Section 7018.5 – Contractors License Law)

THE LAW REQUIRES THAT BEFORE A LICENSED CONTRACTOR CAN ENTER INTO A CONTRACT WITH YOU FOR A WORK OF IMPROVEMENT ON YOUR PROPERTY, HE MUST GIVE YOU A COPY OF THIS NOTICE.

Under the California Mechanic's Lien Law, any contractor, subcontractor, laborer, supplier, or other or entity who helps to improve your property but is not paid for his or her work or supplies, has the right to place a lien on your home, land, or property where the work was performed and to sue you in court to obtain payment.

This means that after a court hearing, your home, land, or property could be sold by a court officer and the proceeds of the sale used to satisfy what you owe. This can happen even if you have paid your contractor in full if the contractor's subcontractors, laborers, or suppliers remain unpaid.

To preserve their rights to file a claim or lien against your property, certain claimants such as subcontractors or material suppliers are each required to provide you with a document called a "Preliminary Notice." Contractors and laborers who contract with owners directly do not have to provide such notice since you are aware of their existence as an owner. A preliminary notice is not a lien against your property. It purpose is to notify you of persons or entities that might have a right to file a lien against your property is they are not paid. In order to perfect their lien rights, a contractor subcontractor, or laborer must file a mechanic's lien with the county recorder which then becomes a recorded lien against your property. Generally, the maximum time allowed for filing a mechanics lien against your property is 90 days after substantial completion of your project.

TO INSURE EXTRA PROTECTION FOR YOURSELF AND YOUR PROPERTY, YOU MAY WISH TO TAKE ONE OR MORE OF THE FOLLOWING STEPS:

Require that your contractor supply you with a payment and performance bond (not a license bond), which provides that the bonding company will either complete the project or pay damages up to the amount of the bond. This payment and performance bond as well as a copy of the construction contract should be filed with the county recorder for your protection. The payment and performance bond will usually cost from 1 to 5 percent of the contract amount depending on the contractor's bonding ability. If a contractor cannot obtain such bonding, it may indicate his or her financial incapacity.

Require that payments be made directly to subcontractors and material suppliers through a joint control. Funding services may be available, for a fee, in your area which will establish voucher or other means of payment to your contractor. These services may also provide you with lien waivers and other forms of protection. Any joint control agreement should include the addendum approved by the registrar.

Issue joint checks for payment, made out to both your Contractor and subcontractors or material suppliers involved in the project. The joint checks should be made payable to the persons or entities which send preliminary notices to you. Those persons or entities have indicated that they may have lien rights on your property, therefore you need to protect yourself. This will help to ensure that all persons due payment are actually paid.

Upon making payment on any completed phase of the project, and before making any further payments, require your contractor to provide you with unconditional "Waiver and Release" forms signed by each material supplier, subcontractor, and laborer involved in that portion of the work for which payment was made. The statutory lien releases are set forth in exact language in Section 3262 of the Civil Code. Most stationery stores will sell the

Figure 10-3 Sample Contract (page 3)

"Waiver and Release" forms if your contractor does not have them. The material suppliers, subcontractors, and laborers that you obtain releases from are those persons or entities who have filed preliminary notices with you. If you are not certain of the material suppliers, subcontractors, and laborers working on your project, you may obtain a list from your contractor. On projects involving improvements to a single-family residence or a duplex owned by individuals, the persons signing theses releases lose the right to file a mechanic's lien claim against your property. In other types of construction, this protection may still be important but may not be as complete.

To protect yourself under this option, you must be certain that all material suppliers, subcontractors, and laborers have signed the "Waiver and Release" form. If a mechanic's lien has been filed against your property, it can only be voluntarily released by a recorded "Release of Mechanic's Lien" signed by the person or entity that filed the mechanic's lien against your property unless the lawsuit to enforce the lien was not timely filed, You should not make any final payments until any and all such liens are removed. You should consult an attorney if a lien is filed against your property."

Each contractor licensed under this chapter, prior to entering into a contract with an owner for work specified as home improvement pursuant to Section 7159, shall give a copy of this "Notice to Owner" to the owner, the owner's agent, or the payer. The failure to provide this notice as required shall constitute grounds for disciplinary action.

Contractors are required to be licensed by the Contractor's State License Board. Any questions concerning a contractor may be referred to the Registrar of the Board, Contractor's State License Board, P.O. Box 26000, Sacramento, CA 95826.

NOTICE TO OWNER OR TENANT: **You may have the right to require Contractor to have a performance and payment bond.**

Figure 10-4 Sample Contract (page 4)

Name and Registration No. of any Salesperson who solicited or negotiated this contract:

Signed this 19 of February 2018.

Signed in the presence of:

_____   _____
Witness   Witness

By: _____   _____
    Name of Owner   Name of Contractor

By: _____   By: _____
    Owner Signature   Contractor Signature

By: _____   _____
    Name of Owner   Street Address

By: _____   _____
    Owner Signature   City/State/Zip

                                      _____
                                      Telephone No.

                                      _____
                                      Contractor's State License No.

Figure 10-5 Sample Contract (page 5)

Contract Items

The contract for home improvements should include the following items:

1 Date of Contract.

2 The contractor's business name.

3 The owner or owners name or names.

4 Full address of the property where the work will take place.

5 The Scope of the Work is a detailed description of the scope of the work to be performed. This should be on a separate sheet or sheets entitled Exhibit A.

6 Reference the plans and specifications, by who designed them, the date of the final drawings and specifications and the designer's project number or drawing number.

7 The approximate start date of the work.

8 The approximate end date of the work.

9 A description of what constitutes substantial commencement.

10 A description of what constitutes substantial completion.

11 The price for the labor and materials to complete the job, the contract price

12 Progress Payments (A payment schedule), including down payment & final payment amounts

13 Who is providing the plans (drawings)

14 Who is obtaining the building permits?

15 A detailed explanation of the contractor's warranty and guarantee for the job and the length of the warranty.

16 Other Terms you want included.

17 Stipulate if any bonds are required, what type of bond or bonds and to what dollar limit.

Require that lien releases be provided to you from all the suppliers, subcontractors, and the general contractor's laborers for work provided up to that point in time.

18 Any penalty clauses.

Figure 11-1 Contract Items

19	Exclusions.
20	A clause stating that the general contractor cannot use any unlicensed subcontractors.
21	A clause that requires that the job be cleaned up at the end of each workday.
22	A stipulation that if arbitration isn't able to resolve your differences that the prevailing party absorb the other's legal fees.
23	A clause that states that the place of litigation shall be in the homeowner's county or parish.
24	An integration clause – this prohibits adding or changing the contract except in limited ways.
25	The name and registration number of any salesperson that solicited or negotiated the contract.
26	Street address, city, state, zip code, phone number, and contractor's license number of the contractor.
27	Signatures of witnesses to the signing of the Contractor Agreement.
28	Signatures of the contractor and the homeowner and date signed.

Figure 11-2 Contract Items (continued)

Bonds

In the construction business there are several types of bonds available, besides the Contractor's License Bond that is required by some states. They are the Performance Bond, Payment Bond, and Contract Bond.

A Performance Bond guarantees the completion of the project according to the plans and specifications. If the job is not completed or is unacceptable, the bonding company can bring in another contractor to finish the job.

A Payment Bond is used to ensure that no liens will be filed against the owner's property.

A Contract Bond ensures that the job will be completed, and all materials and labor will be paid for in full.

If you require the contractor to post a bond, the cost of the bond or bonds will be passed on to you as part of the contractor's overhead. However, it may be worth the peace of mind to have the bond or bonds.

Three-Day Rescission Period

In California, once you sign a contract for your remodel, you may have a three-day period in which to back out of the contract, also called *right of rescission*. Many of us get "buyer's remorse" after making major purchases.

CAL   In California, the homeowner has a three-day rescission period in which they may cancel their agreement with the contractor. Legal Guide K-10 from the California Department of Consumer Affairs states, "Homeowners who enter into contracts with contractors to improve, remodel or repair their homes almost always have a right to cancel the contract, without any penalty or obligation, within three business days after signing the contract."

Three laws have provisions that allow the homeowner to rescind the contract. They are California's post-disaster home-repair provisions, and the California Business and Professions Code section 7163, and the California Home Solicitation Sales Act.

The set of California's post-disaster home repair provisions "automatically voids many contracts for the repair or restoration of a consumer's home signed in the aftermath of disaster."

The California Business and Professions Code section 7163 adds protections to the federal Truth in Lending Act, especially where the contract is not enforceable.

The California Home Solicitation Sales Act allows the buyer, in most consumer transactions that take place away from the seller's place of business and are in excess of $25.00, to cancel the transaction within three business days after signing the contract.

If you secured financing from the contractor to pay for the remodel, the contract is covered under the federal Truth in Lending Act. The federal Truth in Lending Act "provides a three-business-day cancellation period to many buyers in situations where the home improvements are to be financed and involved a security interest in the buyer's home." This law is applicable to all fifty states.

Change Orders

Regardless of how diligent you, the architect, and the contractor have been in detailing the scope of the work to be performed on your project, the unforeseen sometimes arises. It may seem like Murphy's Law at its worst.

For example, at a commercial remodel I ran, the plans called for the breakroom cabinets to be removed and the plumbing moved to the right so the sink could be relocated.

The cabinets were removed. The plumber opened the plumbing wall so he could access the waste and supply lines. The copper supply lines were no problem. The waste line was a mess. It had been jerry-rigged with rubber fittings and was leaking. Also, when he went to turn the water back on after rerouting the supply lines, the shutoff valve was jammed in the closed position and he needed to replace the valve.

Neither of these items was anticipated. They both needed to be fixed. These are instances of when a change must be made to the contract. These changes are called *change orders*. The contractor will determine the cost of the changes, add their overhead and profit, and submit the change order to you for your signature. Since a change order is made a part of the contract, it should be in writing. Once a change order is signed, it becomes a part of the contract as if it had been written into the contract from the beginning.

If a situation arises on your job that requires a change order, It is suggested that you do not let any work covered by the change order proceed until you and the contractor have both signed the change order. Once you and the contractor have agreed to a change order, sign it so work can proceed. It is very annoying to the contractor to have to stop work while waiting for you to sign a change order.

A change order can also be a deduction from the contract. At a residential remodel I ran, the homeowner decided he wanted to hang the drywall himself. A change order was written that eliminated the drywall portion of the project from the contract. That change reduced the contract by $3,000.00 dollars.

Some contractors are "change-order happy." Any deviation from the construction documents will have them writing a change order. Keep in mind a couple things. One, the contractor is in business to make a profit; at least that is the intention. Two, not every deviation from the norm is an excuse for a change order. If the reason for a change order is legitimate and the cost is over $50.00, the change order may very well be justified.

Whether you use the AIA contract, the contractor's contract, or a contract your lawyer has drawn up, the items previously detailed are very important. Make sure that the contract is in writing. Have your attorney review the contract. It will save you time and money.

You can design and create and build the most
beautiful place in the world. But it takes people to
make the dream a reality.

—Walt Disney

Chapter 12. Mechanic's Liens

The *American Heritage Dictionary of the English Language*
defines lien as "the right to take and hold or sell the property of
a debtor as security or payment for a debt or duty."

In most states, mechanic's lien laws were enacted to
protect tradesmen and material suppliers. Mechanic's lien laws
vary from state-to-state. However, their general intent is to
ensure that tradesmen and material suppliers get paid. The
downside of lien laws is that the home may be what guarantees
the payment.

The sidebar at the end of this chapter, "Mechanic's Liens
in California," gives a short description of the basic documents
used in California. Other states will have a variation of this
process.

Some contractors will take advantage of homeowners, subcontractors, and suppliers. Some homeowners try to take advantage of the people and companies who provide labor and material for their construction projects by not paying for that labor and material. You, as the homeowner, must ensure that the suppliers and subcontractors are being paid as work progresses.

To illustrate how the lien process is supposed to work, here is an example, based on California law. Before that, though, we need to discuss Progress and Final Payments. Most contracts for construction should specify a payment schedule. The general contractor invoices the property owner at certain milestones as laid out in the contract. These are *progress payments*. The last payment to the general contractor or to a subcontractor is a *final payment*. A final payment to a subcontractor may come well before the project is complete, but that contractor's work is done. For example, the roofer may be paid in full after the roof is completed but well before the job is done.

In our scenario, the property owner signs a contract with a general contractor. The general contractor should file a Preliminary Notice at this point. (See Appendix Figure A-1.) The general contractor hires an electrical contractor to do the electrical work on the remodel. As soon as the electrician gets the go-ahead from the general, they should file a Preliminary Notice. Each entity that files a Preliminary Notice is also required to file a Proof of Notice Declaration. (See Appendix Figure A-2.) The homeowner should receive Preliminary Notices from every contractor, subcontractor, and material supplier involved in the project. Some of these people won't do it, which impairs their lien rights. As a matter of fact, in California, if an entity does not file a Preliminary Notice, they may not record a lien, even if they do not get paid.

As the framing (carpentry) is nearing completion, the electrician performs the "rough-in" work. The wiring is installed along with any electrical equipment that needs to be inside the walls, such as outlets. When the electrician finishes the rough-in, they invoice the general contractor.

Accompanying the invoice should be a Conditional Waiver and Release on Progress Payment. (See Appendix Figure A-3.) The general contractor should then send their invoice and Conditional Waiver and Release on Progress Payment, a copy of the electrical contractor's invoice, and the electrician's Conditional Waiver and Release on Progress Payment to the homeowner. Once the invoices are paid by the property owner, both contractors should send an Unconditional Waiver and Release on Progress Payment (see Appendix Figure A-4) to the property owner for that portion of the work.

When a materialman (supplier) provides materials for the project, the materialman may sell to a subcontractor who is working on your job. The subcontractor charges the materials to their account. The materialman, on receipt of the order, say, from the electrician, should file a Preliminary Notice. When they invoice the sub who orders the material, the appropriate lien release should be sent as well. These lien releases should be passed on to the homeowner.

As the job nears completion, the electrical contractor returns and finishes the electrical work. An invoice is sent, along with the appropriate lien release. It could be a Conditional Waiver and Release on Final Payment (see Appendix Figure A-5) or an Unconditional Waiver and Release on Final Payment (see Appendix Figure A-6) release. It depends on how the progress payments are structured.

In many cases, the general will withhold 10% of each subcontractor's payment until the very end of the job. This is called "retention" and is used to get the needed subs to return to the job to finish any incomplete work, make any repairs, or fix any equipment that is still outstanding. (See the Punch Lists section in Chapter 15.)

Remember, if a subcontractor performs additional work on the property or the supplier provides additional materials for the project, the process starts all over, for those additional items. This can happen with change orders.

One set of lien releases that is often gets forgotten are those from the general contractor for in-house laborers. The general contractor may use their personnel to do the framing, cleanup, and miscellaneous tasks. General contractors need to provide lien releases for their laborers, just like the subcontractors' laborers. Homeowners should check with an attorney to find other ways to protect themselves.

Examples of the California version of the Preliminary Notice, Proof of Notice Declaration, and the Waiver and Release forms are in the Appendix, Figures A-1 through A-6.

After the final inspection has been passed, a Certificate of Occupancy should be obtained from the building department. This authorizes the property owner to "occupy" the remodeled area(s).

Obtaining the Certificate of Occupancy does not mean all the work is done. Miscellaneous things may need to be completed, such as trim and finishes, and also corrections.

When the property owner is reasonably sure all the work has been completed, the property owner should record a Notice of Completion with the county recorder. While not a part of the lien process, the Notice of Completion sets limits on the time available for a lien to be recorded. In California, once a Notice of Completion has been recorded, a direct contractor has 60 days to record a lien. All others have 30 days to record a lien if they have not been paid.

If a Notice of Completion is not recorded, liens may be recorded for up to 90 days from the last day that work was perform on the project; and that date can be open to interpretation.

CAL   Mechanic's Liens in California

The following documents are the essence of California's Mechanic's Liens for our purposes:

- Preliminary Notice
- Proof of Service
- Lien Release(s)
- Lien

Also, two additional documents factor into the end of the project:

- Certificate of Occupancy
- Notice of Completion

Subcontractors, prime contractors, architects, material supplies (materialmen) and equipment providers are covered by California's mechanic's lien laws. It is in their best interests to file the Preliminary Notice as soon as possible. It is state law that they must file a Preliminary Notice for every job.

The Preliminary Notice informs the general contractor, the property owner, any construction lenders, and any related entities, such as a supplier's supplier. Preliminary Notices should be filed by a contractor or materialman (supplier) when a contract is signed or when they "move" onto the job (start work.) If the notice is filed later than that, the entity filing the notice may lose some protection. For example, if the notice is filed 35 days into the job, the entity loses coverage for the first fifteen days on the job.

The content and layout of the California Preliminary Notice is dictated by the State. The information contained includes

• The name of the entity supplying the labor, materials, equipment or services.

• Their address.

• A description of the labor, materials, equipment, or services being provided.

• The location (address) of the building where the work will be performed.

• The name of the person or company who contracted for the labor, materials,
    Equipment, or services.

• The estimated total price of the labor, materials, equipment, or services.

Receiving a Preliminary Notice does not mean that the named property is about to be sold out from under the property owner. A preliminary notice protects a contractor or materialman's interests. It is the first step to ensuring payment. It also lets all those concerned know that the entity sending the Preliminary Notice is about to provide labor, materials, equipment, and/or services to the named property owner.

Filing a California Preliminary Notice must be done by one of three methods or it does not conform with the law. The methods are they must be hand delivered, delivered by first class, certified or registered mail, or left with a person in charge at the address of the entity to which it is to be delivered.

In addition to filing the Preliminary Notice, the State of California also requires that a California Preliminary Notice **Proof of Service Affidavit** be completed. The affidavit lists the entities to whom the Preliminary Notices were sent, where they were sent, when they were sent, and who sent them. The affidavit attests the sender did in fact do those things stated in the previous sentence.

Each invoice submitted by a subcontractor or materialman should be accompanied by a **Lien Release**. There are four lien releases, each with varying functions. The four types of lien releases are *Conditional Waiver and Release Upon Progress Payment*, *Unconditional Waiver and Release Upon Progress Payment*, *Conditional Waiver and Release Upon Final Payment*, and *Unconditional Waiver and Release Upon Final Payment*.

Conditional Waiver and Release forms declare that the claim against the property owner will be released on the condition of payment of the claim. Unconditional Waiver and Release forms declare that the claim against the property owner has been paid in full and there is no further claim against the property owner.

The homeowner must insist on receiving unconditional releases from all contractors and materialmen once they are finished with the remodel. It is up to the general contractor to make this happen. Conversely, the homeowner is using the contractor's money, so the homeowner should pay on time.

A *Certificate of Occupancy*, which is issued by the building department, allows the remodeled areas to be occupied. Request that the general contractor obtain a Certificate of Occupancy as soon as the final inspection has been passed. While not part of the lien process, a Certificate of Occupancy let's all the parties know that the job is close to completion and it is time to get the outstanding paperwork in order.

Once the job has been finished, the homeowner should record a *Notice of Completion*. This is not a part of the lien process either, but it has an impact on the time contractors and materialmen can record a lien. Prior to recording a Notice of Completion, the property owner must get a Certificate of Occupancy from the building department that issued the building permit. These can be requested once Final Inspection has been passed.

Once the Notice of Completion is recorded, any unpaid subcontractors or suppliers have thirty days to make any claims of mechanic's lien laws or they lose their rights to any claims.

If the work is completed and a Notice of Completion is not recorded, there is a 90-day window for making claims. In the context of the Notice of Completion, recording means the document must be recorded with the county recorder's office. It then becomes a public record.

If a subcontractor or materialman does not receive payment for labor and/or materials provided for the homeowner's job, the subcontractor or materialman has a right to make a claim of mechanic's lien. A *lien* is a legal document recorded with the county recorder. While a lien won't prevent the sale of the property, the lien holder is entitled to be paid from the proceeds of the sale, up to the amount of the lien. Having a lien on real estate may prevent the property owner from refinancing that property.

Much of the discussion on selecting a contractor is designed to prevent homeowners from winding up with one or more liens on their home. If a lien is recorded against the property, property owners should contact an attorney who specializes in lien law as soon as they are made aware of the lien. Other than going to court, the other options for handling a lien are to negotiate a settlement, submit to arbitration, or purchase a bond to cover the lien or liens.

The door handle is the handshake of the building.

—Juhani Pallasmaa

Chapter 13. Paying the Bills

As suggested by the discussion of progress payments in Chapter 10 and mentioned in Chapter 12, the general contractor is due payments at various points of the construction. The ground rules for paying the contractor are:

1. *Never* pay cash for anything.
2. *Never* pay for anything without an invoice.
3. Get a receipt for *everything*!
4. Do not pay any invoice without the appropriate *lien releases!*

Progress Payments

As the project progresses, the general contractor will present you, the homeowner, with invoices for the work completed to date. These payment requests should be in accordance with the payment schedule in the contract.

If, for example, the contract calls for a progress payment for electrical work in the amount of $1,500.00 when the rough electrical is complete, then the electrical contractor's invoice should be for $1,500.00. Accompanying the invoice should be one or more lien releases. The lien releases should be from the electrical contractor and his supplier (materialman) or suppliers.

Remember, anytime the contractor is paid, a receipt must be received! In addition, anything that is included in the contract should be paid to the general contractor, never to any of the workers, subcontractors, and suppliers, with the exception of joint checks.

Joint Checks

If you feel that the contractor is playing games with the finances, joint checks might be a solution. It will also make the subcontractors and material suppliers love you.

In the example above, if the general contractor presents you with an invoice for electrical work for $1,500.00 and if you feel the general contractor is having money problems, you could call the electrical contractor and ask how much was billed to the general for the work so far, excluding materials.

Second, you would ask for the cost of materials installed so far. Ask where the materials were purchased. The difference between the total of the electrician's labor and materials and the general contractor's invoice should be about equal to the general's overhead and profit.

Third, make out two checks. The first one is made out to the general contractor and the electrical contractor for the electrical contractor's labor plus the general's overhead and profit. Then make out a second check to the general contractor and the electrical supplier for the materials plus the general's overhead and profit. You could make one check out to three parties, but that seems to be the limit.

Last, mail or give the checks to the general contractor. The contractor must meet with the electrical contractor and the electrical supplier to cash the checks. The meeting will be at the contractor's bank or at your bank. The bank will cash the checks and give each party the appropriate amount due them. This process ensures the subs and the suppliers get paid on time and in full. The general can't play games with the money, nor stall payment to them.

Payment for Special Orders

In some instances, material that has been specified may be special ordered. Many suppliers require a deposit for special orders. The deposit may range from 10% to 100% of the cost of the special-order item. If the general contractor places the order, this is a valid charge to be passed on to you, the homeowner. To protect yourself, you should make out a joint check to the general and the supplier. Any markup should be paid at the time the material is delivered.

Payments for Change Orders

If a change order is needed for unforeseen work, the contractor may ask for a down payment for the change order. That is fair, to a point. Some contractors want a deposit of 50% for change orders. When the work called for in the change order is finished, they want the balance.

The payment rules mentioned in Chapters 10 and 12 should apply to change orders. Remember that the down payment should be 10% of the change order, unless a large deposit is required for special orders. The balance of the change order should be divided into two payments. One part should be the retention that is paid when the job is done and satisfactory results have been verified. The difference would be total for the change order, less the down payment and the retention.

If a 10% down payment for the change order has been made and 10% retention has been held back, the contractor would be paid 80% when the change order work has been completed. If the change order covers something that takes an extended period of time or involves more than one trade, the homeowner may want to divide the bulk of the payment into two or more progress payments, depending on the total cost of the change order.

Fund Control

If the idea of managing all the money, getting the proper lien releases, paying for change orders, and holding the retention seems too much, for the you, the homeowner, want someone with lots of experience in construction payments handling the progress payments, consider using a fund control company. In the wording of the California version of the Contractor Agreement, *joint control* is used instead of *fund control*. It is the same thing.

Why a fund control company? The fund control company handles all the check writing and bookkeeping. The fund control company acts like an escrow company in a real estate transaction. Fund control is using a third party to disburse the construction funds at prearranged milestones. What are the milestones? The payment schedule set forth in the contract.

To find a fund control company, check with local lumber companies, accountancy firms, general contractors, or lenders, or search on the Internet. Google lumberyards. Look at the listings for local companies. Examine each listing and advertisement for the words *fund control* or *joint control*. You may have to call them directly to verify that they do or do not have a fund control department. You should also Google *fund control.* To the best of my knowledge, none of the large national chains, such as Home Depot, offer fund control.

With Home Depot and Lowes driving many local lumberyards out of business, services such as fund control are harder to find today than they were 10 to 20 years ago. For example, in San Diego County, many fund control companies were established in the mid-1960s. Today, two remain: Dixieline Builders Fund Control, Inc.; and, La Mesa Lumber Fund Control, Inc. Both companies are well respected in the community.

How is a fund control company used? The homeowner fills out a questionnaire about the project. Using that information, the fund control company creates an agreement between them and the homeowner. The agreement spells out the duties of each party, the total cost of the project, the payment schedule and when deposits must be made, and the reports the fund control will provide.

When the homeowner's "fund" is set up, the homeowner gives fund control a list of the contractors and material suppliers and how much each should be paid, and when. Like an escrow, the homeowner deposits funds with the fund control. The fund control, in turn, use the funds deposited to pay the homeowner's contractors and suppliers.

When a payment is due, the homeowner fills out some paperwork, called a voucher. The homeowner gives the voucher to the general contractor. The contractor takes the voucher to the fund control company for payment. The payments that the fund control makes on the homeowner's behalf should mirror the progress payments stipulated in the Contractor's Agreement. The fund control company issues checks to the appropriate parties soon after it has received the vouchers.

If authorized change orders become necessary during the project, payments are not a problem. The fund control companies have forms for increasing and decreasing the amount of money to be paid out. This also handles change orders.

At the end of the project, the homeowner is given a full accounting of the project from the fund control perspective. Using a fund control company may well give the homeowner peace of mind. They make sure that the proper lien releases are submitted. At the homeowner's direction, they will issue joint checks to two and three parties, as needed.

To use a fund control company, the homeowner must have a full cost breakdown from the general contractor that the fund control company can use to pay the proper amounts to the right providers. This gives the homeowner a better sense of the cost of the project.

Using a fund control company will add to the cost of a project, but it may be worth the small cost. If there is a drawback to using a fund control company, it is that fund control companies do not make inspections to verify that the work has been completed.

How do contractors feel about having to go through a fund control company? No contractor should have any objections to fund control. If they have been through the process one time, they shouldn't object. In fact, some contractors would rather deal with a fund control company. The one added complication for the contractor is that they must take one more step to get paid, but they know the check will be good. They don't have to worry about making sure the homeowner has enough funds in his or her bank to cover the checks.

A Few Words of Caution

One tactic is for the contractor to ask for a down payment or deposit of $1,000 and an additional amount for lumber delivery. (It may be for some other material.) Give them the $1,000 and pay them for the lumber when it is delivered, and the lumberyard has provided a lien release.

Never let the contractor get ahead of you. You want a contractor who has a sound enough financial base so that your money is not being used to pay for other jobs, and the contractor can carry several thousand dollars of obligations from one payment until the next. New contractors are known for being poor businesspeople. Fully half the people licensed in 2019 won't be in business five years from when their license went into effect.

Final payment should be no less than 10% of the total price of the contract. This is called retention. Some would suggest a 15% to 20% retention. The smaller the job, the bigger the retention. You want a retention that equates to a large enough amount of money that the contractor won't be tempted to skip out on it.

Payment Worksheet

As suggested above, a file should be kept for the project. One of the things that should be kept is a worksheet that tracks what has been invoiced by the contractor and what has been paid to the contractor. A computer and spreadsheet software make this an easy task to set up so the computer does the arithmetic for you.

In the sample Payment Worksheet in Figure 12, there are places to log all the progress payments, called *draws* in the construction industry, and the amount of each. *(This worksheet, as well as other worksheets and checklists, is available in full-size format at no cost, from PeterAKlein.com.)* Each time a payment is entered into the Amount Paid column, the Current Balance is adjusted. Using the worksheet gives a current balance and provides a place to record the invoice numbers, check numbers and dates paid for the entire project.

Paying for a remodel is more than just writing checks to the general contractor. You, the homeowner, must make sure the subcontractors and suppliers are being paid and that the proper lien releases are being received. The homeowner needs to know when to write joint checks or make use of a fund control company.

Payment Worksheet

Job Name: _____
Job Address: _____

Item No.	Invoice No.	Date Submitted	Date Received	Check No.	Item	Item Amount	Amount Paid	Current Balance	Due Sub	Sub Name
1					Base Contract	$0.00		$0.00		
2					Deposit	$0.00	$0.00	$0.00		
3					Change order	$0.00	$0.00	$0.00		
4								$0.00		
5								$0.00		
6								$0.00		
7								$0.00		
8								$0.00		
9								$0.00		
10								$0.00		
11								$0.00		
12								$0.00		
13								$0.00		
14								$0.00		
15								$0.00		
16								$0.00		
17								$0.00		
18								$0.00		
19								$0.00		
20								$0.00		
21								$0.00		
22								$0.00		
23								$0.00		
24								$0.00		
25								$0.00		
26								$0.00		
27								$0.00		
28								$0.00		

Figure 12 Payment Worksheet

The bitterness of poor quality remains long after the
sweetness of low price is forgotten.

—Benjamin Franklin

Chapter 14. Construction Defects

Even in the best of circumstances, things may go wrong. Some of the problems may be very subtle. The difference between right and wrong may be a few inches in 20 feet. This is difficult for most people to see. In this chapter we'll look at construction defects, touch on the causes of construction defects, and explore how they may be resolved.

What is a Defect?

Construction defects are the things that go wrong during the construction of a structure. Construction defects range from minor to catastrophic. A painter's using the wrong color is a minor, though annoying, defect. The failure of the Tacoma Narrows Bridge in 1940 was a major defect.

A construction defect can be a deviation from the plans and specifications, or it can be a poor design. For example, if the architect specifies a solid-core door between the house and the garage, which is code, and the contractor installs a hollow-core door, that is a defect. The contractor deviated from the plans and specifications. It is an easy problem to correct, but it is wrong.

To illustrate a defect, here is a real-world example. My partner and I were laying out the walls on a new house after the slab had been poured and finished. The front wall of the house was neither parallel nor perpendicular to any of the other walls. We doublechecked the plans and the other walls we had laid out. We scratched our heads a bit. Then it hit us.

The slab was one and one-half inches shorter on one side of the house than the other. We both had experience setting form boards for concrete. We realized that one side of the house was the proper dimension from front to back. The reason, one of the form setters had held the tape measure against the rear form board on one side of the house. On the other side of the house, the end of the tape had been hooked over the form board. The thickness of the form board is one and one-half inches!

Here is a list of common defects:

- Wrong size door or window
- Door or window in wrong place
- Improper installation of a door or window

- Wall in the wrong place
- Wall wrong size – length, thickness or height
- Improper material, finish or color
- Defective material
- Defective, sloppy or improper workmanship

An example of poor or defective design might be the plans calling for a specific material to coat the outside of an exterior wall that is partially buried on one side. The coating is supposed to keep moisture from penetrating the wall. The coating is installed as per the plans and specifications and the wall leaks. That is a design defect.

How Do Defects Happen?

One term that needs definition is *scaled.* Scaled means using a tape measure to measure a dimension on the plans and then converting that distance into feet and inches. If the plans are drawn at ¼" to the foot (¼" : 1'-0") and the worker measures $2^1/_{16}$", the measurement must be converted to the proper feet and inches. In this example, $2^1/_{16}$" on the plans is equal to 8'-3" on the property.

Most construction workers will do the math in their heads in less time than it took you to read the previous paragraph. Sometimes mistakes are made. In my experience, people's misreading dimensions on the plans or scaling causes many construction problems.

For most home remodels, construction defects can be traced to a lack of supervision. This tends to point to the general contractor. David Rawls, owner of Struct-One in Imperial Beach, California, says that when the contractor, the project manager, or the job superintendent is on the job all the time, the mistakes go way down. Mistakes are being made, but the supervision is there to catch and correct the mistakes. As a contractor's business grows, the contractor can't be on each job all day, every day. As the contractor and the key field personnel get spread thinner and thinner, the mistakes keep occurring, but no one is catching them.

If you, the homeowner, discover a problem, one key to resolution is bringing the problem to the contractor's attention as soon as discovered. If it is discovered that a window or door is the wrong size or in the wrong place after the drywall has been hung and taped, it is going to take more to fix it than discovering the problem while the walls are still open. This is one reason you are urged to walk the remodel every day and be familiar with the plans.

A change of mind by the homeowner is not a construction defect. It is a mental lapse on the homeowner's part. If you change your mind, don't expect the contractor to absorb the cost of making the change.

One other note about changes: they may require resubmission to the building department. That in turn can slow down or stop the project and increase costs.

While the framing was going up on one of my own remodels, my wife wanted to add a window. It would have cost us two to three weeks, additional architect's fees, and an additional permit fee. That doesn't include the cost of the window and the framing. We figured the window would cost us $1,000. If we could just put it in, it would have been about $600, but then we would have violated a law. The window never went in.

Prevention vs. Remediation

Construction-defect litigation has become big business in the legal profession over the past three decades. It is a bigger problem for builders of condominiums and housing tracts than for custom homes and remodels. What can be done to prevent construction defects? And if you have defects, what do you do?

Above all else, the ideal is to prevent construction defects. It is more cost effective and easier to make changes to the plans than to the house. Getting a good set of detailed plans is the best thing that can be done to ensure what is desired is what is built. Then, pick a good contractor. Next, make sure the contract for the work references the plans and mirrors the work as laid out in the plans.

If problems are discovered early on, it is easier and cheaper to fix them at that time than to fix them days, weeks, months or years later. If a problem (defect) is discovered during construction, it should be brought to the general contractor's attention as soon as possible. The earlier a problem is identified, the easier and more economical it is to fix.

What's in the Contract?

If a conflict arises between you as the homeowner and the contractor, the first place to look for resolution is in the plans, the specifications, and the contract. If the point of contention is in the contract documents, then the resolution is that the point of contention should be completed as spelled out in the contract.

If the point of contention is not covered in any of the contract documents, odds are that the contractor does not have to do it, plain and simple. Therefore, the plans, specifications, and contract should be very detailed. The more detail, the less chance of things going wrong or not being done. This is another reason you need to be involved with day-to-day supervision or to do at least a daily walk-through.

If the point of contention is of an interpretive nature, you may have to bring in a neutral third party to render a decision. By using an architect or building designer, you have someone with the expertise to make an impartial decision. Another option is to call a different architect who has no interest in your job.

The architect will charge for their time, but it could save a lot of time and money.

Dollars and Common Sense

If a difference of opinion arises with the builder over some aspect of the remodel, how hard should you push for resolution? If the problem is a valid one and it concerns the structural integrity of the house, the watertight integrity of the house, any health or safety issue, or the finish of the remodel, don't give up until the problem has been resolved in the proper way. That is what is being paid for.

If it is something that is not going to be seen and doesn't affect the structural integrity of the house, the watertight integrity of the house, any health or safety issue, or the finish of the remodel, and is of nominal cost to fix, forget it. Save your energy for things that matter.

As the construction takes place, make sure the various components are of the size, shape, and location called out in the plans. As mentioned previously, learn to use a tape measure and read the plans.

On occasion, you may notice something that has been in place for a while and seemed like it was as it should be. Then one day you take another look and realize something is amiss. Let's say you were having a fancy medicine cabinet installed.

Because you are tall, you want the top at a certain height. And it isn't. Was the height noted on the plans? Was the height conveyed to the contractor? Was the installed height assumed? Where should the fault lie? You must work it out with the contractor. It may not be defect but an oversight on your part.

Despite the best efforts of those involved, things sometimes go wrong. Most times these errors are unintentional. People make mistakes. Your job is to get the error corrected.

Sometimes an issue will arise that the parties can't resolve. Both sides feel sure about their positions, and neither party wants to budge. An outside architect has been brought in, and neither side likes the architect's proposed solution. Then what? When the parties are at loggerheads, three stages or levels of legal action are available. They are mediation, arbitration, and litigation. Let's look at each of them, in order of cost.

Mediation

The first thing to try is mediation. With mediation, both sides meet with a neutral third party. The mediator has been trained to look at both sides and remain impartial. The mediator may or may not have any legal experience. The mediator may or may not have any experience with cases involving construction.

Both parties should carefully and thoroughly consider the mediator's recommendation. A lot of time and money will be saved by resolving the issue at this juncture. Mediation comes down to the parties' deciding the outcome with help from the mediator.

However, unless the contract has language that requires the parties to abide by the mediator's decision, either party may disagree with the mediator's decision and choose arbitration or litigation.

Arbitration

In most contracts, there is a provision to submit to arbitration. Arbitration is the key here. Unless the contractor absconds with the money or in some other manner breaches the contract, don't bother to sue. Arbitration is much faster and cheaper than litigation.

Most of us have heard the term *binding arbitration* used in conjunction with labor disputes. It may be a case where the president calls on labor and management to return to the bargaining table and try to work out an agreement. If they can't, the president may call for binding arbitration.

A third party is brought in as the arbitrator. The arbitrator listens to both sides and renders a decision. In arbitration, the decision is binding in most cases. Arbitration can be completed in much less time than litigation.

Another benefit of arbitration is that the arbitrator will be dispassionate and not emotionally involved. Know that the decision of the arbitrator may not be appealed.

Litigation

A problem with filing a lawsuit is that the legal process has a lot of built-in delays. In legal terminology it is called *discovery*. Discovery is the time spent researching the facts of the case, taking depositions, and researching case law. Discovery can delay the litigation for months or longer. The duration of discovery can be very frustrating to both sides.

Remember, if you pushed for the litigation, your lawyer is trying to find every facet of the case that will help your side. Litigation can take longer than the actual construction.

If the claim is for $10,000.00 or less, in California, you can use Small Claims Court. Small Claims Courts are designed for non-lawyers. The California Contractors State License Board (CSLB) pamphlet *A Consumer's Guide to Filing a Smalls Claims Court Construction Claim* does a good job of explaining the preliminary work the claimant must do and how the CSLB may be able to help the claimant collect if they prevailed in Small Claims Court. The pamphlet outlines how to name defendants, the contractor, and related businesses. Many Small Claims cases are resolved in just a few months.

Litigation can take years to resolve. Your goal as the homeowner should be to get the issue resolved and the remodel finished. If you opt for litigation, be prepared to wait.

Unlike mediation or arbitration, a lawsuit may wind up before a jury. A jury can become very emotional. Lawyers play to the jurors. Are hyped-up jurors in your best interest? Also, the losing party pays court costs. Jury cost starts at $15,000.

An old building is like a show. You smell the soul of
the building. And the building tells you
how to redo it.

—Cameron Mackintosh

Chapter 15. Ending the Project

It will happen at last. The remodel is done. This is the day you have been waiting for since planning the remodel first started. Some things need to be done before the remodel is complete.

Final Inspection

When the project is substantially done, the contractor will call the building department for the final inspection. The building inspector will come to the house to walk through the remodeled area. If the inspector sees anything that doesn't comply with the building code, a correction notice will be issued. The contractor will have the appropriate trade(s) make the correction or corrections and call for re-inspection.

Certificate of Occupancy

Once the final inspection has been passed, you or the contractor should go to the building department and get the Certificate of Occupancy. This certificate means that it is all right to occupy the remodeled premises. This is a paperwork step for the most part. Give the building department a couple of days to get the final inspection on file before requesting the Certificate of Occupancy.

Punch Lists

Passing the final inspection and securing the Certificate of Occupancy do not mean that the job is done. There could very well be some odds and ends to complete. It also does not mean you are ready to make the final payment.

It is now time for the white glove inspection, the homeowner's white glove inspection! You should make an appointment with your contractor or the contractor's superintendent to compile a final punch list. This is the last chance to point out any deficiencies to the contractor. It is the contractor's job to correct the deficiencies in a reasonable amount of time.

During this walk-through to compile the final punch list, be super picky because this is the last chance to get anything corrected that is not of major nature, such as a leaking pipe. If the contractor or superintendent is excellent in customer service, they will point things out that they won't accept, in addition to the items you listed.

The entire job should be covered, inside and outside. You should look at each surface slowly, methodically. Try to find something wrong. Don't forget to look at the ceiling and floor in each room. Look at each wall, the floor, and ceiling from different angles and positions. It is a good idea to walk the job without the contractor, a day or two before the joint inspection. That way it can be done at your pace, without feeling rushed.

I would also suggest that you perform a couple of walk-throughs, on your own, at times of the day that are different from when you walk through with the contractor. Different light conditions can show different things. Be sure to write down these findings.

Some of the things to look for are bows in walls, irregular wall and ceiling textures, areas with gaps in the painted surfaces, countertops that are not smooth and level, cabinet doors that are not square to the rest of the cabinet, and uneven gaps, top to bottom, between doors and their door frames. Are there gaps where cabinets meet walls? Make sure the fit of doors and windows is snug and that they open and close easily. Are the joints in baseboards and other moldings mitered and smooth? Are all electrical outlets hot? Are all lights working? Does hot water come out of the hot side of faucets, and cold out of the cold side? Pay special attention to tile work, such as countertops and floors. Make sure they are level in all directions, adjusting for drainage if appropriate. Can a large can slide on its side without catching the edge of a tile?

Has the landscaping been cleaned up, and have any and all holes and trenches been filled in? Also, make sure the contractor has done a complete cleanup of the job, inside and out, and removed all their equipment, supplies, and debris. A clean job is a happy job—and a safe job.

This is not an exhaustive list, but it gives a start to things to look for.

Documentation

If any type of equipment or appliance was installed as part of the project, the contractor should give you any and all owner's manuals and warranties. You should also receive the building inspection job card and the approved set of plans. At this point, you should have lien releases from every subcontractor, supplier, and laborer who has had anything to do with the job. No manuals? No releases? no payment!

Get a list of the all subcontractors who worked on the project. You may find the plumber to be someone you may contact for service calls if needed later on.

You should also get a copy of the As-uilt plans. This is a set of plans that has been marked up in red to indicate deviations from the original approved plans. These deviations could be due to change orders or building inspections.

Final Payment

Once all the documentation has been delivered to you, the punch-list items have been corrected, final inspection has been signed off, and the Certificate of Occupancy issued, now—and only now—is it time for the final payment to be made. Make sure the appropriate lien releases have been received from the contractor at the appropriate times in relation to when the final payment is made.

Notice of Completion

This is the time to record a Notice of Completion to further protect the property from liens. The Notice of Completion should be recorded after the work has been finished and no work has been performed on the job for several days.

The process involves completing the Notice of Completion form and having it recorded with the county recorder. It is something you, the homeowner, can do.

Certificate of Acceptance After Final Inspection

Some contractors may ask to have a Certificate of Acceptance After Final Inspection signed by the homeowner. This certificate, when signed by both homeowner and contractor, stipulates that the homeowner has inspected the job and that there are no outstanding issues. It ends the job for the contractor.

If the builder has satisfied all the items mentioned in this chapter, including lien releases, documentation, and punch-list-item completion, this is a valid document and ends the job. If you have any reservations about the project, don't sign this certificate. Once it is signed, there is no recourse.

If the contractor wants you to sign one of these certificates and you are not ready, take the form and tell him you'll sleep on it. This should defuse the situation for a day or two. At some point, you will have to explain why you aren't comfortable signing the certificate.

When It's All Over

The job is done, the workers have all moved on to other projects, and the furniture is in place. *It's over!*

One thing to keep in mind about construction is that it is rough work with large tolerances. It is not like building a piano. You are going to find that not everything may have been done as expected, but it does comply with the plans and specifications. Some areas may not wear as well as others. Unless there are serious problems, these are minor things that you should accept.

Afterword

A lot has been covered in this book. We started out figuring out what to build, selecting materials, setting a budget, looking at the costs of a remodel, and financing the remodel. We looked at selecting an architect and what to expect from one, and then we spent a lot of time talking about selecting a contractor. We delved into building permits, the items you should include in the contract, and what happens during the construction process. We finished up with paying the bills, mechanic's liens, resolving differences, and ending the project. Now it is up to you. It is time for you to put these lessons to good use and undertake your remodel.

Start and continue the process of educating yourself about remodeling. Read about the construction and remodeling process. You can find several good books on home remodeling in your local library.

One caution: Many of the books available in libraries may be outdated or regional in scope. Barnes and Noble has many good books. Books along the lines of this book, as well as books that describe how to do things such as electrical work, may be worth reading—not so you can do the work, but so you have a rough idea of the process.

New materials, new equipment, new tools, and new methods keep entering the building trades. Thirty years ago, nail guns were mostly used for nailing off plywood on roofs and walls. Today, nail guns are used for most nailing tasks. Twenty years ago, drywall was nailed to the studs and joists. Currently, drywall is attached to the walls and ceilings with screws driven by electric screw guns.

Keep in mind that what works in New England may be different from what works in California. Lots of exterior wood trim may weather well in Maine but will twist and look bad after a few summers in the Southwest desert.

Unless you are a hard-core do-it-yourselfer, you will not be doing the work yourself; but you should get a rough idea of how things are done. Learn to read plans. Price materials. As with any endeavor, the more knowledgeable you are about remodeling and construction, the better off you are, and the less likely you are to be taken advantage of by a contractor.

Avoiding conflicts of interest is an important part of protecting yourself. Using a contractor to secure a loan for your remodel, using the design services of your contractor, or using a friend or family member as your contractor may not work to your advantage.

It has been said before: if something seems too good to be true, it probably is. Don't get greedy. Expect and demand quality workmanship from the contractor, and expect to pay a reasonable price for the remodel, which includes a reasonable profit for the contractor.

Let's look at the goal that was set at the beginning of this book: for you to become aware of strategies for a successful home remodel.

I think that goal has been met. No one can cannot guarantee that if you read this, or any other book on remodeling, problems won't crop up during your remodel. You should be in a better position to keep from becoming the victim of an unscrupulous contractor or supplier. You should be able to select a good contractor and write a solid contract. You should be able to watch the job and have a basic idea of what is happening. You should be able to control the money to keep the contractor from getting ahead of you. Resources have been provided for you that you may use to further your education of the construction process. If you do that, we have met our goal.

Remember, you have allies in your research. Allies at your disposal are your lawyer, your accountant or tax specialist, your insurance agent, the mortgage holder for your home, friends who have remodeled their homes, your state's consumer affairs department, your state's contractor licensing agency, and the Better Business Bureau. Use them.

One word regarding the Better Business Bureau: just because a contractor is not a member does not mean they should be excluded from the list of possible contractors. Membership can be expensive, and many contractors would rather put that money into other things.

I wish you success with your remodel and enjoyment of the finished product!

Acknowledgments

I would like to thank the following individuals for the time they took to provide information, review the text, or point me in the right direction. This book couldn't have been written without you.

Diane Marie Forster Dennis, Construction-Business-Forms.com, Tumwater, WA; Rosemarie Litoff, C2 Reverse Mortgage, San Diego; Andy Cruz, Business Consultant, Chula Vista;[10] Mike Sullaway, Sullaway Engineering, San Diego; Walter Goodseal, Urban Design Group, Chula Vista; Clayton DeKorne, Chief Editor, JLC Group, Washington, DC; Glenna Bloemen, Vanderblümen Publishing, La Mesa; Peter Lapsiwala, Permits & More, San Diego; Rosemarie Litoff, C2 Financial Corp., San Diego; and Bonnie Baranoff, Front Matter Marketing, La Mesa.

---

[10] All cities are located in California unless otherwise stated.

Peter Harn, Fudge's Carpets & Drapes, El Cajon; Jeri Hess, Century 21 Award, La Mesa; Ski Knowles, Dixieline Lumber, National City; Matt Mauzy, President, Mauzy Heating and Air Conditioning, El Cajon; Patricia Nelson Miller, President, Dixieline Builders Fund Control, Inc., San Diego; David Rawls, Owner, Cutting Edge Builders, Imperial Beach; Lauri Riley, First Financial Services, El Cajon; Siegfried Rothfuss, Architect, Cutting Edge Builders, Imperial Beach; Sandi Smelik, Century 21 Award, La Mesa; and Grace Wasan, La Mesa Lumber Fund Control, Inc., La Mesa.

Appendix. Mechanic's Lien Form Examples

Each state has its own version of the forms used for Mechanic's Liens. The six examples used in *15 Steps to a Successful Remodel: How to Survive the Process* are from Construction-Business-Forms.com and are the California versions of the forms. They include the following:

A-1. Preliminary Notice

A-2. Proof of Notice Declaration

A-3. Conditional Waiver and Release on Progress Payment

A-4. Conditional Waiver and Release on Final Payment

A-5. Unconditional Waiver and Release on Progress Payment

A-6. Unconditional Waiver and Release on Final Payment

These forms may not be copied nor used without permission from Construction-Business-Forms.com. The forms may be purchased directly from Construction-Business-Forms.com.

A special thank you to Diane Marie Forster-Dennis at Construction-Business-Forms.com for all her help.

PRELIMINARY NOTICE
(In accordance with California Civil Code Sections 8034, 8100, 8116, 8200, et seq.)
PRIVATE WORKS PROJECTS

NOTICE TO PROPERTY OWNER

EVEN THOUGH YOU HAVE PAID YOUR CONTRACTOR IN FULL, if the person or firm that has given you this notice is not paid in full for labor, service, equipment, or material provided or to be provided to your construction project, a lien may be placed on your property. Foreclosure of the lien may lead to loss of all or part of your property. You may wish to protect yourself against this by (1) requiring your contractor to provide a signed release by the person or firm that has given you this notice before making payment to your contractor or (2) any other method that is appropriate under the circumstances. THIS NOTICE IS REQUIRED BY LAW TO BE SERVED BY THE UNDERSIGNED AS A STATEMENT OF YOUR LEGAL RIGHTS. This notice is not intended to reflect upon the financial condition of the contractor or the person employed by you on the construction project. If you record a notice of cessation or completion of your construction project, you must within 10 days after recording, send a copy of the notice of completion to your contractor and the person or firm that has given you this notice. The notice must be sent by registered or certified mail. Failure to send the notice will extend the deadline to record a claim of lien. You are not required to send the notice if you are a residential homeowner of a dwelling containing four or fewer units.

_____ **is the claimant on this notice.**
(Enter name of actual claimant here)

The claimant's estimated demand, if any, after deducting all credits and offsets will be in the amount of
$ _____

A general statement of the work provided:
_____
_____

Description of the job site sufficient for identification (including the street address of the site if any):
_____
_____

OWNER (or Reputed Owner)   DIRECT CONTRACTOR
_____   _____
_____   _____
_____   _____

CONSTRUCTION LENDER (if any)   OTHER (if any)
_____   _____
_____   _____
_____   _____

Name & Address   Name of person/firm that contracted to
of person giving   purchase the labor, service, equipment,
this notice and   and/or materials:
his/her/its
relationship to
the claimant:
Is person giving this notice a claimant? ☐ YES ☐ NO
Signature _____
Date _____

California 20-Day Preliminary Notice Form for Private Works Projects
www.Construction-Business-Forms.com – Copyright 2012-2019 Monk and DBug, LLC

Figure A-1. Preliminary Notice

PROOF OF NOTICE DECLARATION
California Civil Code Section 8118

Per California civil code the undersigned served copies of the California 20-Day Preliminary Notice form for Private Works projects:

☐ By personally delivering the notice to the person or the persons to be notified

☐ By registered, certified mail, or express mail; or overnight delivery by an Express Service Carrier

☐ By leaving the notice and mailing a copy in the manner provided in Section 415.20 of the Code of Civil Procedure for service of summons and complaint in a civil action

As evidenced by the following:

☐ Attached documentation provided by the United States Postal Service showing that payment was made to mail the notice using registered, or certified mail, or express mail

☐ Attached documentation provided by an express service carrier showing that payment was made to send the notice using an overnight delivery service

☐ Attached return receipt, delivery confirmation, signature confirmation, tracking record, or other proof of delivery or attempted delivery provided by the United States Postal Service, or a photocopy of the record of delivery and receipt maintained by the United States Postal Service, showing the date of delivery and to whom delivered, or in the event of non delivery, by the returned envelope itself

☐ Attached tracking record or other documentation provided by an express service carrier showing delivery or attempted delivery of the notice

On: _____ at: _____
     (Date Notice Served)   (Time Notice was Served)

Names and Addresses of Parties Served

Owner (or reputed Owner)	**Direct Contractor**
_____	_____
(Owner or Reputed Owner)	(Direct Contractor Company Name)
_____	_____
(Name of Person Served)	(Name of Person Served)
_____	_____
(Title of Person Served if applicable)	(Title of Person Served if applicable)
_____	_____
(Street)	(Street)
_____	_____
(City, State, Zip)	(City, State, Zip)

Construction Lender (if any)	**Other (if any)**
_____	_____
(Lender Company Name if applicable)	(Other Company Name if applicable)
_____	_____
(Name of Person Served)	(Name of Person Served)
_____	_____
(Title of Person Served if applicable)	(Title of Person Served if applicable)
_____	_____
(Street)	(Street)
_____	_____
(City, State, Zip)	(City, State, Zip)

I declare under penalty of perjury under the laws of the State of California that the foregoing is true and correct.

_____   _____
(Signature of person who served notice)   (Title of signer)

_____   _____
(Name of company that signer represents)   (Printed or typed name of signer)

Signed at _____ , California, on _____ , 20_____
                    (City and/or County)   (Month and Date)   (Year)

California 20-Day Preliminary Notice for Private Works Projects Proof of Notice Declaration
www.Construction-Business-Forms.com - Copyright 2012-2019 Monk and DBug, LLC

Figure A-2. Proof of Notice Declaration

CONDITIONAL WAIVER AND RELEASE
ON PROGRESS PAYMENT

California Civil Code Section 8132

NOTICE: THIS DOCUMENT WAIVES THE CLAIMANT'S LIEN, STOP PAYMENT NOTICE, AND PAYMENT BOND RIGHTS EFFECTIVE ON RECEIPT OF PAYMENT. A PERSON SHOULD NOT RELY ON THIS DOCUMENT UNLESS SATISFIED THAT THE CLAIMANT HAS RECEIVED PAYMENT.

IDENTIFYING INFORMATION

Name of Claimant: _____

Name of Customer: _____

Job Location: _____

Owner: _____

Through Date: _____

CONDITIONAL WAIVER AND RELEASE

This document waives and releases lien, stop payment notice, and payment bond rights the claimant has for labor and service provided, and equipment and material delivered, to the customer on this job through the Through Date of this document.

Rights based upon labor or service provided, or equipment or material delivered, pursuant to a written change order that has been fully executed by the parties prior to the date that this document is signed by the claimant, are waived and released by this document, unless listed as an Exception below.

THIS DOCUMENT IS EFFECTIVE ONLY ON THE CLAIMANT'S RECEIPT OF PAYMENT FROM THE FINANCIAL INSTITUTION ON WHICH THE FOLLOWING CHECK IS DRAWN:

Maker of Check: _____

Amount of Check: $ _____

Check Payable to: _____

EXCEPTIONS

This document does not affect any of the following:

(1) Retentions.
(2) Extras for which the claimant has not received payment.
(3) The following progress payments for which the claimant has previously given a conditional waiver and release but has not received payment:
Date(s) of waiver and release: _____
Amount(s) of unpaid progress payment(s): $ _____
(4) Contract rights, including:
(A) a right based on rescission, abandonment, or breach of contract, and
(B) the right to recover compensation for work not compensated by the payment.

SIGNATURE

Claimant's Signature: _____

Claimant's Title: _____

Date of Signature: _____

Job/Acct # (if app.) _____

Figure A-3. Conditional Waiver and Release on Progress Payment

**UNCONDITIONAL WAIVER AND RELEASE
ON PROGRESS PAYMENT**
California Civil Code Section 8134

NOTICE TO CLAIMANT: THIS DOCUMENT WAIVES AND RELEASES LIEN, STOP PAYMENT NOTICE, AND PAYMENT BOND RIGHTS UNCONDITIONALLY AND STATES THAT YOU HAVE BEEN PAID FOR GIVING UP THOSE RIGHTS. THIS DOCUMENT IS ENFORCEABLE AGAINST YOU IF YOU SIGN IT, EVEN IF YOU HAVE NOT BEEN PAID. IF YOU HAVE NOT BEEN PAID, USE A CONDITIONAL WAIVER AND RELEASE FORM.

IDENTIFYING INFORMATION

Name of Claimant: _____
Name of Customer: _____
Job Location: _____
Owner: _____
Through Date: _____

UNCONDITIONAL WAIVER AND RELEASE

This document waives and releases lien, stop payment notice, and payment bond rights the claimant has for labor and service provided, and equipment and material delivered, to the customer on this job through the Through Date of this document. Rights based upon labor or service provided, or equipment or material delivered, pursuant to a written change order that has been fully executed by the parties prior to the date that this document is signed by the claimant, are waived and released by this document, unless listed as an Exception below.

The Claimant has received the following progress payment: $_____

EXCEPTIONS

This document does not affect any of the following:

(1) Retentions.
(2) Extras for which the claimant has not received payment.
(3) Contract rights including:
(A) a right based on rescission, abandonment, or breach of contract, and
(B) the right to recover compensation for work not compensated by the payment.

SIGNATURE

Claimant's Signature: _____
Claimant's Title: _____
Date of Signature: _____
Job/Acct # (if app.) _____

Figure A-4. Conditional Waiver and Release on Final Payment

CONDITIONAL WAIVER AND RELEASE
ON FINAL PAYMENT

California Civil Code Section 8136

NOTICE: THIS DOCUMENT WAIVES THE CLAIMANT'S LIEN, STOP PAYMENT NOTICE, AND PAYMENT BOND RIGHTS EFFECTIVE ON RECEIPT OF PAYMENT. A PERSON SHOULD NOT RELY ON THIS DOCUMENT UNLESS SATISFIED THAT THE CLAIMANT HAS RECEIVED PAYMENT.

IDENTIFYING INFORMATION

Name of Claimant: _____

Name of Customer: _____

Job Location: _____

Owner: _____

CONDITIONAL WAIVER AND RELEASE

This document waives and releases lien, stop payment notice, and payment bond rights the claimant has for labor and service provided, and equipment and material delivered, to the customer on this job.

Rights based upon labor or service provided, or equipment or material delivered, pursuant to a written change order that has been fully executed by the parties prior to the date that this document is signed by the claimant, are waived and released by this document, unless listed as an Exception below.

THIS DOCUMENT IS EFFECTIVE ONLY ON THE CLAIMANT'S RECEIPT OF PAYMENT FROM THE FINANCIAL INSTITUTION ON WHICH THE FOLLOWING CHECK IS DRAWN:

Maker of Check: _____

Amount of Check: $_____

Check Payable to: _____

EXCEPTIONS

This document does not affect any of the following:

Disputed claims for extras in the amount of $_____

SIGNATURE

Claimant's Signature: _____

Claimant's Title: _____

Date of Signature: _____

Job/Acct # (if app.) _____

California Conditional Waiver and Release On Final Payment (#3 Lien Waiver/Release Form)
www.Construction-Business-Forms.com – Copyright 2012-2019 Monk and DBug, LLC

Figure A-5. Unconditional Waiver and Release on Progress Payment

**UNCONDITIONAL WAIVER AND RELEASE
ON FINAL PAYMENT**

California Civil Code Section 8138

NOTICE TO CLAIMANT: THIS DOCUMENT WAIVES AND RELEASES LIEN, STOP PAYMENT NOTICE, AND PAYMENT BOND RIGHTS UNCONDITIONALLY AND STATES THAT YOU HAVE BEEN PAID FOR GIVING UP THOSE RIGHTS. THIS DOCUMENT IS ENFORCEABLE AGAINST YOU IF YOU SIGN IT, EVEN IF YOU HAVE NOT BEEN PAID. IF YOU HAVE NOT BEEN PAID, USE A CONDITIONAL WAIVER AND RELEASE FORM.

IDENTIFYING INFORMATION

Name of Claimant: _____

Name of Customer: _____

Job Location: _____

Owner: _____

UNCONDITIONAL WAIVER AND RELEASE

This document waives and releases lien, stop payment notice, and payment bond rights the claimant has for all labor and service provided, and equipment and material delivered, to the customer on this job. Rights based upon labor or service provided, or equipment or material delivered, pursuant to a written change order that has been fully executed by the parties prior to the date that this document is signed by the claimant, are waived and released by this document, unless listed as an Exception below.

The Claimant has been paid in full.

EXCEPTIONS

This document does not affect the following:

Disputed claims for extras in the amount of: $ _____

SIGNATURE

Claimant's Signature: _____

Claimant's Title: _____

Date of Signature: _____

Job/Acct # (if app.) _____

Figure A-6. Unconditional Waiver and Release on Final Payment

References

American Institute of Architects. AIA.org.

Becker, Norman. *The Complete Home Inspection Handbook.* New York: McGraw-Hill Book Co., 1980.

Better Business Bureau. BBB.org.

California Architects Board. CAB.ca.gov.

California Architects Board. *Consumer's Guide to Hiring an Architect.* Sacramento: California Architects Board, 2019.

California Contractors State License Board. *Home Improvement Contracts: Putting the Pieces Together.* Sacramento, CA: California Contractors State License Board, 1999.

California Contractors State License Board. *What You Should Know Before You Hire a Contractor.* Sacramento, CA: California Contractors State License Board, 1999.

"Cost vs. Value Table." *Remodeling Magazine.* 2019. Remodeling.hw.net/cost-vs-value/2019/.

Forster-Dennis, Diane Marie. Mechanic's Lien Forms. Tumwater, WA: Construction-Business-Forms.com, 2012.

Hanley Wood, LLC. *Remodeling Magazine* (in general). Washington, DC: Hanley Wood, LLC.

Irwin, Robert. *The Home Remodeling Organizer.* Chicago: Real Estate Education Co., 1995.

Investopedia. 2020. Investopedia.com/terms/n/nonrecoursedebt.asp.

Local Building Departments: Google the name of the jurisdiction where the property is located, such as Spokane. Many websites for governments have the .gov suffix. Click on the government website link. Once there, use the website's search function to find the planning and building departments. Some may be called something like Development Services. When you have found the department you want, you may call them to see if your questions may be answered over the phone. If not, verify the address. Some planning/building departments are not located in city hall.

Luxenberg, Susan Diamond. *Fearless Remodeling*. Rochester, NY: Homesmart Consulting, Inc., 1999.

*Philbin, Tom. *How to Hire a Home Improvement Contractor Without Getting Chiseled*. New York: St. Martin's Griffin, 1996.

RehabLoanNetwork.com. 2019.

State of California. Contractors License Board. CSLB.ca.gov.

U.S. Department of Housing and Urban Development. HUD.gov.

Glossary

This glossary lists words and phrases that are commonly used in construction. My experience has been in Southern California; a different word or phrase may be used in other parts of the country

ABS	A black plastic used for plumbing pipes.
AGC	Associated General Contractors.
Angle stop	The valve used to turn the water on/off to a toilet.
Backfill	Fill placed back into an excavation, such as a trench.
Beam	A heavy horizontal bearing member, made of wood or metal.
Bearing wall	A wall that bears the weight of the roof and/or floors above the ground floor.
BIA	Building Industry Association.
Breaker	A device installed in an electrical panel that is designed to turn off or "break" in the event of an overload on that circuit. Also called a circuit breaker.
Brown coat	The second coat of stucco or plaster on the exterior of a building.
Butts	Hinges.
Camber	A surface having a slight slope or angle. In construction, a piece of lumber may have a camber to prevent water from pooling.
Cased opening	An opening, usually a doorway, without any trim on either side of the opening.
Casing	The trim around a door opening.
Chase	A closed-in pathway for ducts, pipes, or wires.
Check	A defect in lumber characterized by gouge in the surface that could impact its structural integrity.
Chink	A defect in lumber characterized by a portion of a flat surface that has a camber.
Color coat	The third coat of stucco or plaster to a building. Colored powders are added to the stucco as it is being mixed.

Condensate	Water that collects when a cold refrigerant is passed through a fan unit in an air conditioning system.
Condensate line	A line that carries condensate from a forced air unit to a place where it can be collected or dispersed.
Conduit	Pipe used to protect electrical wiring.
Cripple	A short stud above a door or above or below a window.
Crown	The curvature of a piece of lumber from end to end along the short dimension. Lumber should always be installed crown up.
Cup	The curvature of a piece of lumber from side to side along the wide dimension.
Dead load	The weight of an element that never moves; i.e., the pole, the wall, column, and floor of the building.
Deadbolt	A door-locking device that has a key on one side and a thumb lever on the other. Some have a key on both sides—a double deadbolt.
Device	Refers to electric switches, outlets, and other finish trim.
Disconnect	A heavy-duty electrical switch used for machinery. In residential construction, disconnects are used at air conditioning units.
Dormer	An area of the roof that is raised above the surrounding area.
Eave	The area under the roof between the outside of the building and the edge of the roof.
Embed	Any metal device used to connect the foundation to the framing. The devices are embedded into the concrete while the concrete is wet so that the concrete hardens around the device.
Entry lockset	A lock for a door that needs to be locked and requires a key to unlock it from the outside. A Nest- or Ring-brand lock also qualifies as an entry lockset.
Face frame	The front frame of a cabinet. The drawers and door close against the face frame.
Fish tape	A long, stiff metal tape used to "fish" wires through conduit.
Flashing	Sheet metal used to keep water from entering a dry area. Typically seen around pipes that penetrate the roof.
Furring	The wood or metal used to level a floor of wall.
Gable	A wall under the roof where the roof is an upside-down V shape.

Hanger	A metal device attached to a vertical surface, such as a wall or foundation that holds a framing member perpendicular to the wall. May be called a *joist hanger.*
Hardware, door	The mechanism used to keep a door closed or to open it. See *Passage hardware, Privacy lock, Entry lockset,* and *Deadbolt.*
Hardware, general	Any device used in construction to tie two things together.
Header	The heavy lumber that carries the weight across the top of a door, window, or other opening in a wall.
Hip	A roof that angles up on three or four sides.
Hold down	Any of a variety of metal objects embedded in the concrete foundation of a building and attached to the walls to hold them down.
ICC	International Code Council, the organization that writes building codes.
Jamb	The frame of a doorway.
Jamb stock	The material used to finish a doorway. The door is hung on the jamb stock.
Joist	A horizontal framing member that supports a floor or a ceiling. In flat roofs, it will also support the roof.
King studs	The studs that support the header of a door or window opening.
Lath	A metal mesh applied to walls that will receive a covering of plaster or stucco. The mesh may come attached to building paper. The plaster or stucco is troweled into the lath during the first of the three coats.
Lien	A legal document file to ensure that those providing labor or materials get paid.
Live load	A live load is the weight of something that can be moved, for example, an item of furniture, a person, a car or truck, or even a box of stuff in storage, as that can be moved.
Main panel	The box where the electric meter and main breakers are located.
Mansard	A roof style with a steep slope above the perimeter walls of a building and an open area over the rest of the building. More often used in commercial buildings to hide roof-mounted equipment.
Mast	The metal pipe that extends above a roof; the pipe contains the wires supplying electrical service to a building.

MDF	Multi-dimensional fiberboard, a man-made board that is good for cabinetry and certain other applications where plywood doesn't provide a decent finish.
Mesh	A metal or plastic screen or fabric.
Metal framing	Building frames made from metal members instead of wood members. More common in commercial buildings than in residential buildings.
Miter	A cut made so that two pieces of material may be fitted together snugly, end-to-end.
Mud, concrete	The wet concrete.
Mud, drywall	Compound applied to cover nails and adhere tape to joints.
Mud, stucco	The wet stucco before it is applied to the building.
Mullion	The wood or metal dividers in a window.
Non-bearing wall	A wall that bears no load or weight from above.
Orange peel	Light texture applied to interior walls.
OSB	Oriented strand board. Looks like a sheet of plywood but is created via different process. OSB is stronger than plywood.
P/T valve	Pressure and temperature valve on a water heater. If the pressure or temperature in a water heater exceeds the manufacturer's limits, the P/T valve opens to relieve the excess. This valve should have a copper pipe running from it to a point where the hot water can be discharged safely.
Passage hardware	Door hardware that has no locking mechanism.
Pier	A support sticking out of the ground, onto which other things will attach.
Pitch	The slope of a roof, expressed as a fraction or ratio such as 4/12. This is read as 4 in 12. This means that the roof rises 4 feet for each 12 feet of horizontal run.
Plate	A wood or metal framing member at the top or bottom of a wall.
Plumb	Straight up and down, not leaning in any direction.
Plumb and line	To straighten the walls of a building after they are framed. Plumbing the walls ensures that they are straight vertically. Lining the walls ensures that they are not bowed or curved.

Power wash	A high-pressure washing of the exterior of a building.
Pressure treated	A process that impregnates lumber with chemicals so the lumber will not deteriorate when it comes into contact with concrete.
Privacy lock	Door hardware that may be locked for privacy but does not have a key. Often used for bathrooms and bedrooms.
R value	Pertains to the quality of insulation. A higher value indicates thicker insulation, which stops more temperature transfer.
Rafter	A roof framing member installed at an angle above the outside walls.
Riser	The vertical portion of a set of stairs.
Schedule	1. The planned work of a project plotted against time. 2. A list on a set of plans that details the doors, windows, and/or finishes of rooms of a project.
Scratch Coat	The first of three coats of stucco.
Setback	The area between the property line and buildable area of a lot.
Shear panel	Plywood nailed to the exterior of a wall, with the long dimension aligned vertically, that prevents a building from racking during high winds and earthquakes.
Shot	A special nail that is used to secure lumber to concrete or masonry. The nail is placed in a special gun and shot into the wood and concrete, hence the name *shot*. The shot, also called the *pin*, is powered by a .22 caliber blank.
Sill	The bottom ledge of a window. Also, may be used to refer to the bottom of a wood wall.
Simpson	A manufacturer of metal ties to hold pieces of lumber together or to hold lumber to concrete or masonry.
Sinker	A nail used in framing that has a green vinyl coating.
Slab (slab on grade)	The foundation, consisting of concrete poured on the ground, which also serves as the building's floor.
Sprayed acoustic texture	A texture sprayed on interior drywall ceilings. Also called cottage cheese.
Square	1. A tool used to ensure perpendicular cuts; may also be used to make angled cuts for roofs and stairs. 2. A term indicating that two adjoining surfaces are perpendicular to each other.
Stop	The trim piece inside a door opening that stops a door from swinging through to the other side.

Strap	Thin, narrow band of metal.
Stucco	The plaster applied to the exterior of a building. In most cases it is applied in three layers or coats.
Stud	A vertical framing member in a wall.
Style	The members that form the frame of a door.
Sub-panel	A secondary set of circuit breakers at a different location than the main panel.
Tape	A solid paper or plastic mesh tape applied over the joints of drywall.
Teco	A type of small nail used for nailing lumber to specialized metal ties; used to hold two pieces of lumber together.
Tongue and groove (T & G)	Lumber that has a groove along one side and a lip on the other side. The tongue of one-piece fits into the groove of another.
Tread	The parts of a set of stairs where you put your feet.
Truss	A prefabricated floor or roof structural component.
Tub/shower enclosure	The glass door and glass walls that close the open sides of a tub or shower.
Tub/shower surround	The material the covers the walls of a bathtub or shower. It can be ceramic tiles or plastic one piece.
Tyvek	"DuPont™ Tyvek® HomeWrap® is the original house wrap, incorporating unique material science that helps keep air and water out, while letting water vapor escape." This wrap goes over the framing and under the exterior finish such as plaster or siding.
Valley	The low point of a roof where two roof planes come together. A valley carries runoff to the roof edge, a drain, or gutter.
Vent	A plumbing pipe that runs from a plumbing fixture through the roof. The vent lets odors escape and provides air so liquids can flow to the sewer.
Waste Pipe	The pipes that carry the outflow of plumbing fixtures to the sewer.

Index

ABC, 82
Accessory Dwelling Unit, 34
ADA, 69
aesthetics, 39, 52, 53, 54, 74
AGCA, 82
Aging in Place, 69
American Institute of Architects (AIA), 48, 168, 238
approved plans, 151, 162, 222
arbitration, 108, 167, 214, 215, 216, 217
architect, 12, 13, 15, 20, 29, 42, 43, 44, 45, 46, 47, 48, 49, 64, 82, 83, 122, 137, 145, 149, 150, 158, 159, 183, 208, 211, 212, 214, 224
asbestos, 128, 129, 130
As-Builts, 151
Associated Builders and Contractors, 82
Associated General Contractors of America, 82
balloon payment, 26
barrier-free shower, 69
Better Business Bureau, 94, 227, 238
BIA, 82
bidding, 83, 105, 141
Bidding, 101, 105, 106
Bids, 108

bonds, 97, 181, 182
Borrow from Life Insurance, 21
Bringing Residences Up to Code, 165
budget, 12, 13, 14, 15, 18, 19, 40, 41, 42, 44, 224
Budget, 11
Building codes, 156, 158
building department, 5, 15, 47, 91, 141, 143, 147, 150, 151, 155, 158, 159, 160, 162, 165, 166, 190, 211, 218, 219
building departments, 66, 143, 144, 155, 156, 158, 162, 239
Building Industry Association, 82
Building inspectors, 163
building permit, 8, 36, 41, 70, 143, 147, 153, 155, 158, 159, 166
cabinets, 17, 29, 30, 34, 57, 112, 117, 147, 153, 183, 184, 220
CAD, 47, 49
California, 4, 9, 15, 34, 35, 39, 44, 50, 56, 57, 58, 59, 61, 62, 67, 68, 72, 76, 80, 81, 84, 89, 91, 92, 93, 95, 110, 120, 137, 143, 153, 156, 159, 160, 168, 171, 182, 186, 187, 190, 200,

About the Author

Peter A. Klein lives in the San Diego, California area. He is a Navy Vietnam veteran, served on the board of directors of the Vietnam Veterans of San Diego (now Veterans Village of San Diego), and  as a Veterans Resource Coach at the Veterans Resource Center in San Diego's Central Library.

Peter has a daughter and two sons. He likes swimming, reading, and model railroading. He is a speaker and freelance writer, and he also teaches classes about remodeling.

About the Cover Artist

B. Asher Klein is a visual artist and graphic designer based in San Francisco, California. He earned a bachelor's degree in Illustration at the Academy of Art University of San Francisco. See more of his designs at BAsherK.com.

CPSIA information can be obtained
at www.ICGtesting.com
Printed in the USA
LVHW010343260820
664160LV00003B/355

9 781734 034301